The author grew up on a farm in rural western Massachusetts. He worked his way through college, majoring in chemical engineering. A career in military, aerospace, government programs and industrial products followed, which included working at all levels of engineering and management.

Because of his broad base in high performance materials and process techniques, he has extensive capabilities at resolving challenges in a variety of demanding applications.

Recovering from a life-changing accident, he started a new career as a writer. By combining his diversified background and experience at solving problems, he was able to provide unique approaches to writing mysteries. Here, he describes the technological advances he made possible in aerospace and several diverse industries.

Contributions of George Dahlquist at NBHS, and Homer D. Reihm (Sonny) at ILC Dover in getting me started on my career path are acknowledged with thanks.

To: Eileen

Tim Parker

Tim Parker

TOUCH DOWN

"The Eagle has landed!"

AUSTIN MACAULEY PUBLISHERS™

LONDON • CAMBRIDGE • NEW YORK • SHARJAH

A CIP catalogue record for this title is available from the British Library.

ISBN 9781528951067 (Paperback)
ISBN 9781528972956 (ePub e-book)

www.austinmacauley.com

First Published (2020)
Austin Macauley Publishers Ltd
25 Canada Square
Canary Wharf
London
E14 5LQ

Natalie Spinetti had sufficient patience and provided encouragement throughout the composition process.

Thanks goes to Sue Strelow for her inputs and her diligent efforts in checking spelling and punctuation.

Jerry Parker helped explain and correct the problems with the '*&#@^' computer word processing along the way.

Table of Contents

Table of Figures

Preface

In a writers' workshop, I submitted a short essay on my aerospace contributions in helping to put men on our moon and have them returned safely to Planet Earth. I was surprised by the amount of interest generated, as the other members of the group were considerably younger.

It hadn't occurred to me that many of them weren't around for the first lunar landing by the Apollo 11 Mission crew. I was floored when they pointed out that for them, this was history. When I stopped to think about it, in 2019 it will be 50 years since men first walked on the moon in July of 1969. It almost seems like it was only yesterday. It is really astonishing that there still are people who claimed the trips into space and to the moon were all faked on a movie set somewhere.

One mother of a five-year-old boy was anxious to learn about how I became an aerospace engineer/rocket scientist. Apparently, she was extremely interactive with her son and worked with him constantly to make sure he had all the age appropriate toys and games that he could learn from and be challenged by them. Although I tried to be as helpful as I could, it felt like she wanted to clone a younger version of me with her son.

This memoir explains how to become an aerospace engineer or rocket scientist at a time when classes and information to accomplish either didn't exist. The examples contained herein are intended to demonstrate how someone can tackle any new problem or challenge, even when it is outside their comfort zone or area of expertise. With creative thinking, use of one's entire background and experience enables technology transfers between fields of application to adapt square pegs to fit in round holes (or how to get to the moon and back).

Starting off in chemical engineering, I did more engineering, materials development and processing than chemistry early in my career. Many problems and product development approaches were resolved by working with suppliers to determine how to use their products. Discussions with customers or government agencies helped to find out what was needed for their applications.

My job descriptions in the space programmes evolved from the race to space with the Russians. They were beating us on every step into the cosmos. We were afraid that left unchecked, they could rain missiles and rockets down on us from Earth orbit or a base on the moon.

There was neither a blueprint on what we were trying to do nor instructions available on how to accomplish it. Basically, I had to use everything I had learned on the farm, in school and all my part-time jobs to figure out how to help the astronauts get from point E (Earth) to point M (moon) and back unscathed. Because it was unchartered territory, every step of the way was a challenge, a lot of fun and a very rewarding experience.

So where does one go when the space programme slows down due to lack of funding? Besides the fulfilment of reacting to the challenges of programmes, demands and solving problems, one wants to assure that one's family is well provided for.

When sales, marketing and product managers were being paid more than technical people, I switched to doing that instead. As a business and product line manager, I usually didn't have sufficient technical support, so I ended up performing that function as well. Eventually, I became a general manager and president of a small company. I was good at handling the business aspects, but it wasn't fun, just paperwork. I ended up as technical director in product line management as well as doing research and development where I could be more creative again.

For the most part, in my day schools didn't teach students how to think. School primarily consisted of memorising things that were too soon forgotten. I had a science teacher named George Dahlquist in high school who would say, *"The man who said it couldn't be done was rudely awakened one morning by the sound of someone doing it."*

I assume that was a shorter version of Edgar Albert Guest's poem* from over 100 years ago:

It Couldn't be Done*

Somebody said that it couldn't be done,
But, he with a chuckle replied
That "maybe it couldn't," but he would be one
Who wouldn't say so till he'd tried.
So he buckled right in with the trace of a grin
On his face. If he worried he hid it.
He started to sing as he tackled the thing
That couldn't be done, and he did it.

Somebody scoffed: "Oh, you'll never do that;
At least no one has done it";
But he took off his coat and he took off his hat,
And the first thing we knew he'd begun it.
With a lift of his chin and a bit of a grin,
Without any doubting or quiddit,
He started to sing as he tackled the thing
That couldn't be done, and he did it.

There are thousands to tell you it cannot be done,
There are thousands to prophesy failure;
There are thousands to point out to you one by one,
The dangers that wait to assail you
But just buckle it in with a bit of a grin,
Just take off your coat and go to it;
Just start to sing as you tackle the thing
That "couldn't be done," and you'll do it.

On military and aerospace programmes, I was one of the many who did what '*they*' said couldn't be done. It was easy for me to think outside the box, because I never learned how to think inside the box. I was assigned projects where in-the-box thinkers didn't know where to begin.

Lightly metallized deposits of aluminium on film used for microwave heating, electrostatic discharge (micro lightening) protective packaging and thermal control for buildings supposedly "*oxidizes rapidly after exposure to air*" according to industry experts. Plotting electrical conductivity vs optical opacity tests changes to verify aluminium deposition thickness, I demonstrated that didn't happen.

"*Ultrasonic cleaning of computer chips causes damage*" was the mantra of the electronics industry. The same people thought a yield of 40% (throwing out 60% of product produced) was a good yardstick as an industry standard. That was until I determined that higher power ultrasonic to be a better way to discover defective parts and reduce fracture failures at the end user, while producing a cleaner product faster.

To arrive at the point where my skills could be perpetually helpful to most firms involved a continuous learning process. I always applied what I learned working on school vacations at a dozen different part-time jobs. Often those lessons were just as useful as what I had learned in industry. Likewise, what I had done in military and aerospace programmes served me well in commercial enterprises later on. Many people stop learning new things at the start of their careers or only look for answers within their narrow specialty. I explored every possibility that came to mind from my prior experience to solve each new problem or challenge. That's how I became a '*Jack of all trades*' and willing to tackle anything.

In 1994, my son Paul Parker presented me with a book entitled **MOON SHOT** by astronauts Alan Shepard and Deke Slaton. Inside the front cover he wrote:

"Dad, I hope that this book will bring you back to the time when you first achieved your goals. A time when the future was spread out widely before you, and an entire nation shared with you a sense of pride in your accomplishments.

Though I have had only a few all too fleeting glimpses of that kind of success, and the satisfaction that must have meant to you at that wonderful time of your life!

With the past freshly renewed in your mind, I hope that you will have a better perspective from which to view where I stand at this point in my life. That's why it is imperative that I continue to strive to achieve my goals.

Thank you so much for the support that you have given me at this difficult time in my life. It has been invaluable.

Merry Christmas Dad,
With love & admiration to you always,
Paul"

Inside the back-cover of the book, Paul quoted President Calvin Coolidge on Persistence:

"Nothing in this world can take the place of persistence.
Talent will not; nothing is more common than unsuccessful people with talent.
Genius will not; unrewarded genius is almost a proverb.
Education will not; the world is full of educated derelicts.
Persistence and determination alone are omnipotent."

That kind of sums up what it took to get to the moon along with the efforts of about 400,000 Americans doing their part.

Mysteries by Tim Parker include:
WISPA
MISSING in Switzerland

Notes:
1. **Names have been changed to protect those accused.**
2. **Photographs courtesy of National Aeronautics and Space Administration.**

Chapter 1
Lunar Touch Down Press Briefing –
July 1969

Somehow, as a guy from a small New England town who ultimately became an aerospace engineer, I found myself centre stage before the Apollo 11 launch in 1969 for the first lunar landing. Standing in front of a myriad of press microphones and cameras under the hot lights at Cape Canaveral in Florida, I explained what a spacesuit was and why it was necessary to protect the astronauts from the hostile environments of space and the lunar surface.

(Figure 1) Apollo PGA

In government parlance, the spacesuit was called a Pressure Garment Assembly (Fig. 1 – PGA). An Integrated Thermal Micro-Meteoroid Garment (Fig. 2 – ITMG) is worn on top of the PGA for additional protection. At this joint press briefing, DuPont's corporate marketing people were there to field questions on their high-performance materials developed for use in the Apollo Manned Space Program to get astronauts to the moon and returned safely. It was flattering that I was selected as the best my company and NASA had to explain why the suit materials were developed and what they had to do.

(Figure 2) PGA/ITMG

I was astonished to see so much interest expressed by the international journalists. If their enthusiasm had been bottled, the excess energy could have supplied the Saturn V rocket with an extra boost off the Kennedy Space Center launch pad. Due to their excitement, the foreign press couldn't seem to ask enough questions. Many scribbled notes as fast as possible, but most extended their arms with tape recorders through the sea of flashbulbs to not miss a titbit of information.

On the other hand, the US reporters were totally blasé about the whole aerospace programme. Jules Bergman, who was the Science Editor for *ABC News* exemplified this ho-hum attitude. He seemed to feel his role was to be the designated critic as he badmouthed the design of what he referred to as the big, bulky, cumbersome spacesuits we 'inflicted' on the poor astronauts. It didn't seem to occur to him that these independent units were the best available at providing the options of breathing and functioning in the vacuum of space and on the moon. Having invested many long hours to ensure astronaut survival in extreme environments, I was tempted to take a swing at him to wipe the smug look off his face.

(Figure 3) Apollo 11 Lunar Module

Because of the negative slant of the domestic media coverage, the nation didn't seem to appreciate the risks involved to these test pilots turned astronauts. Captain Pete Conrad was a Navy test pilot and an aeronautical engineer who had flown every conceivable type of experimental aircraft. He was considered to be one of the best we had. With a perfect descent and ascent of the lunar module (Fig. 3) to and from the command module orbiting above, there was only a two percent margin of error on fuel. He told me, *"That thing has me scared shitless."* Coming from Pete, that comment really surprised me.

Conrad was fully aware that NASA had decided early on that a back-up rescue mission launched from Earth would not have any better probability of success than the original attempt and would only endanger more lives.

In the initial NASA plan, the lunar module needed to fly up to at least a hundred miles above the moon to meet the command module for the trip home rather than risk the life of the third astronaut as well.

Pete became the third man to walk on the moon in the Apollo 12 Mission. At 5'6", he was one of the shorter astronauts. As he stepped off the ladder on the Lunar Module, he joked, *"Whoopee! Man, that may have been a small one [step] for Neil, but that's a long one for me."*

22

Because of the high risks involved, the lunar module was eventually retrofitted with a bigger engine and redesigned to reduce weight. In later landings, the Command Module Pilot was allowed to come down to within ten miles of the moon to retrieve the astronauts in the Lunar Module as it blasted off the lunar surface for the return flight home. The original concern was the lack of knowledge on how high the mountains on the moon might be.

Many people in this country reflected the bored media view and wondered why we were 'wasting money' going to the moon even though the peak spending on NASA programmes was less than four percent of the federal budget to counter the perceived Soviet threat that existed since Sputnik (the first Russian satellite). The fear was that the USSR could establish manned stations in Earth orbit and on the lunar surface.

In forty years, the NASA funding average had been well under one percent of the national budget. The rapid advances in computers, science, medicine, electronics, construction, transportation, weather forecasting, defence and materials that were a direct result of the aerospace effort haven't been fully recognised by the media nor the public in general.

These developments put the United States light years ahead of where we would have been otherwise. MRI Global (Midwest Research Institute) concluded the economic impact of the $25 billion total invested in the space programme between 1958 and 1969 had a payoff of $181 billion by 1987 or a seven-dollar return for each dollar spent.

Because it took 40 pounds of fuel to get a pound of payload into orbit, parts were miniaturised. Mainframe computers that once took up large rooms have been functionally replaced by calculators and multipurpose phones that can fit in your pocket. Tiny pressure transducers developed to monitor astronauts' heartbeats and respiration rates in flight are now threaded up veins to determine if patients have valve problems or holes between chambers without the necessity of open-heart surgery.

In the earlier programmes, the spacesuits were custom fit: so the astronauts looked like Buck Rogers (Fig. 4). Unfortunately, when they were put in environmental chambers to replicate the thermal extremes in space and on the moon (-250°F to +330°F), the suit occupants overheated or froze.

(Figure 4) Early spacesuits

Multiple layers of reflective films interleafed with porous fabric spacer layers were required to obtain protection from both the intense heat and the frigid cold. Otherwise the astronaut would boil on the side of the suit facing the sun and freeze his butt off on the shady side. Because this appearance led to Jules Bergman's "*bulky and cumbersome*" comments about the spacesuits, a test subject was filmed throwing and catching a football in an Apollo suit to demonstrate the flexibility.

The suits also were modified to envelop the astronaut in circulated oxygen to equalise the temperature around the body. A set of thermal cotton underwear (long John's or 'a union suit') was interlaced with 360 feet of vinyl tubing to become the Liquid Cooling Garment (LCG). The LCGs have been adapted for extreme industrial applications, such as working on blast furnaces to pour steel.

As much as I wanted to, I couldn't stay at Cape Kennedy for the launch of Apollo 11 that would make the first lunar landing on July 10, 1969 (Fig. 5). My son was in an oxygen tent at the hospital back in Dover, Delaware, so I had to rush home.

For each mission cycle in space, I had to be within an hour's driving distance of Cape Canaveral, Houston's Manned Space

Center or the company's headquarters in Delaware. NASA was serious about key people being available for emergencies.

(Figure 5) Apollo Saturn V

One time they called from Houston on a Saturday when I was up on the roof of my two-story house. They insisted I come downstairs immediately for a conference call. That's the problem when you're considered indispensable, you don't have time to train a replacement.

In a launch photo, the Saturn V rocket (363 feet tall) can be seen in Fig. 5. The moon (target) was 240,000 miles off. Because of programme demands, I never did get to see a launch until Apollo 17 the last voyage to the moon. I was on vacation, so I had to keep checking in and stayed in the area. From a mile and a half away across Indian River, the roar was louder than a dozen freight trains bearing down on the viewing stands. The ground shook as if it was a major earthquake until the Apollo Saturn V Rocket was well above the launch pad. The vibrations felt like they could have easily registered a seven or an eight on the Richter scale while they rattled my rib cage.

So, at the tender age of 26, how did I end up speaking at Cocoa Beach (Cape Canaveral) for the launch of our first trip to land on the moon with the Apollo 11 mission?

Chapter 2
Farm Growing Up

(Figure 6) North Brookfield Farm

Far removed from the glow of urban lights, a poor farm boy could be seen in the hills of central Massachusetts searching the night sky in awe. Lying in the soft hay, the moon and the Milky Way seemed so close I could have reached up and touched them. I had no idea that someday I'd play a role in not only helping people escape Earth's gravity to achieve orbit, but to reach the moon in four days and then return safely to Planet Earth.

I had a rather auspicious start to life in February of 1943. The evening of my birth at home in a 250-year-old farmhouse coincided with the beginning of a lunar eclipse on a clear night. That could have been an omen foretelling of my eventual link to the moon. On the other hand, maybe it was an ominous warning to my parents that they might be in trouble with this kid.

Exactly how did one become an aerospace engineer anyway? Of course, there was no such thing back in the 1950s. It started from age five with a mother who insisted that every quarter earned for mowing a lawn, clearing the snow off a neighbour's driveway and delivering newspapers be saved for college (whatever that was). Working full time on weekends and school breaks from the age of nine added to the fund. I was surprised that I needed a Social Security Number when I was that young to work in a local apple orchard.

Like all struggling young farmers, Dad made do with what he had to compensate for the government subsidised mega-sized farms in the Midwest that drove up the price of grain and limited the amount he could grow for his own use. Government price restrictions on poultry, eggs and meat as well as high taxes on farm property in Massachusetts didn't help either. That's why most of the farms in New England have disappeared and water taken from the Colorado River to irrigate the deserts in California supply the Northeast with produce that is no longer grown here.

Small farmers like my father were getting taxed out of existence when most support or tax breaks for farms were going to large corporations in the Great Plains states, California and the Midwest. Dad left school in the eleventh grade to help support his family. He went back to night school to take math courses to become a machinist to work full time and try to keep the farm going like my uncles did on theirs.

Dad would borrow equipment from neighbouring farms at times. A few hand tools, such as hammer, saw, block and tackle, were used to reassemble a barn addition from materials he had taken apart from an unused barn in town. We never had a power tool before I was a teenager. At age four or five, my job was to pull the nails from the old wood and straighten them for reuse.

My dad had a fantastic baritone voice and was always singing with a smile or whistling while he worked. While we were taking down the barn in town, he would sing 'Too Fat Polka' that Arthur Godfrey sang on the radio in 1947. Another song I remembered him singing a lot was 'Hoop-Dee-Doo' sung by Perry Como in 1950.

A large pry bar was a modified car axel obtained from a local blacksmith. Cutting off the back of a Model A Ford sedan and adding a wooden platform on the back to make a truck allowed him to move the lumber and pick up grain and supplies from the railroad depot in town.

Hard work wasn't something learned. Mum helped instil a work ethic from birth. You picked up after yourself; washed the dishes; fed and cleaned up after the animals; milked; collected the eggs; mowed the lawn and weeded the garden or you didn't get any dessert. Nothing complicated about that. There was never a question, *"Can I do something?"* Whatever needed to be done, the unstated answer to the unasked question would have been, *"I can."*

When I was tall enough to reach the top of the kitchen woodstove that had been converted to kerosene, I cooked my breakfast in a single egg poacher from the age of four. At that time, there was no government agency to say I was too young to do that. I couldn't reach over the rim of the enamelled cast iron farm sink to do dishes, so I used a step stool (without a seat belt). My three brothers and I each had to weed one row of vegetables in a half-acre garden every day. The nice part was that we could munch on a carrot or a pea pod while we crawled from one end of the garden to the other. It was always a relief to reach the end of a row.

My brother Russ (five years older) would get frustrated with me when I would pretend to be fishing in a mud puddle in our dirt road at the foot of the hill after a heavy rain. He would stamp his feet and say for the umpteenth time, *"There are no fish in the puddle."* That always would evoke a big grin on my part. He was usually upset because I was always making up what he called *"fish stories"*. Some people are no fun at all.

Ultimately, Russ would later work on classified computers in the Air Force before settling down to programme mainframes for major industrial and retail companies up and down electronics row (firms along the inner Boston belt way formerly known as Route 128 now I-95) for a living.

As a munchkin, we didn't have kindergarten, but with two older brothers I'd watch what they were doing for schoolwork. That's probably why I had no trouble passing a test to get in first grade early at five years old.

Being close in age to Jerry, we were more like twins, doing everything together. He did enjoy sleeping in more than I did. I'd drag him out of bed at daybreak to open up the range shelters in the field for the chickens. The shelters would protect the chickens from foxes, weasels and skunks at night. They could

28

run around inside the fenced in field during the day. Would that make them cage free or free ranged? That seems to be important nowadays. Do chickens have feelings too? There was one Rhode Island Red I named Henrietta. It didn't matter which coop she was put in at night, she always got free and greeted me when I opened up the shelters in the morning.

Much to the chagrin of my mother, Jerry and I were always doing something together that she would get upset about. We'd climb up to the tops of tall skinny ash and birch trees. Once we got them swinging back and forth, we'd each grab the other tree and switch as we passed each other.

Usually when we were doing something dangerous, I'd get blamed not only for what I did, but for what Jerry did too. He was the 'good' kid who could do nothing wrong. Jerry was usually smart enough not to admit he was involved. I still have the scar on my knuckle from holding a broad burdock leaf into the reel blade of a lawnmower while Jerry was pushing it. We were trying to see how it worked.

When we were little tykes, we decided to dig a hole out by the barn to see if we could get to China. We were making excellent progress once we got down to the drainage rocks for the barn. Dad came out and got upset. He filled the hole back in.

Sometimes it seemed Mum had no sense of humour. I learned she didn't like snakes when I brought home a six-foot black water snake from a fishing expedition at the creek over the hill. I wanted to keep it for a pet, but she chopped off the head with a hoe and I had to bury it.

Mum said the first fish we caught was too small to cook, but she fried it anyway. So, she was a good sport after all.

Being born and raised in a now 300-year-old house had its advantages. Most of the tools in the tool bin under the workbench in the tool shed were at least 100 years old. No one complained when we kids figured out how to use them to build things. There were no instructions offered and plenty of experimentation to learn as you go. That was the beginning of my training in problem solving, design and invention.

Mr Benvenuti had a fruit and grocery store in town. From time to time he would have an extra wooden orange crate available. It was amazing what could be built in the tool shed from the thin and thick boards. At the age of four or five, I wanted to make something for my dad on Fathers' Day. I cut two triangles from the thick ends and added two sides, so it resembled a pup tent. Putting a cleat on a sloping side to hold the heel of a shoe in place, it became a shoeshine stand. I found a rusty can of deep maroon oil-based paint in the shed and got it painted before dark. The next day the paint was still wet, but he wasn't upset as he cleaned the paint off his hands with kerosene.

For a Cub Scout project, I cut down an ash sapling and used a drawknife with the tool shed vice to shave the nodes from the branches smooth. Cutting a notch in one end, I used twine from the hay bales to lace in a wooden spear point I had made on the end of the seven-foot pole. Painting bands of blue and yellow (Cub Scout colours) on the shaft and adding a few chicken feathers completed the project.

There was a mound of dirt near the crab-apple tree remaining from digging out for the base of the barn addition. The goats liked to climb to the top and we used it to play 'King of the Mountain'. Standing on top of the pile with my new spear I told my younger brother Ron to start running. He was a fair distance away when I threw my new weapon. Not wanting to hurt him, I aimed for his feet, but I took a chunk out of his calf with the spear point. Ron healed up fine, but the episode probably added a few more grey hairs to my mother's head.

Jerry seemed to work harder in school than everyone else just to keep up. Having a younger brother who didn't appear to be doing any homework assignments was probably discouraging too. When we did get a guidance counsellor at our high school, he recommended that Jerry apply to a small, unaccredited college in Vermont. Fortunately, the suggestion was ignored.

Eventually Jerry was able to stay current with his assignments through perseverance and excelled after high school. Graduating at the top of his class in electrical engineering at Lowell Tech, he spent 30 years at IBM making computers before he was induced to accept a generous early retirement package he couldn't refuse. Having read a couple of papers he wrote at the corporate office; I was impressed and proud he had come so far on his own. He reinvented himself and switched to software engineering management for his second career.

When I was five years old, Russ pawned off seven of his newspaper customers on me because they were spread out over five miles. I would have to walk a lot faster on the way home from school on the days I was given detention for what I considered were minor infractions. Usually I was talking in class because I was bored to tears.

On the paper route, there was a German Shepherd who was friendly when he wasn't drunk. Unfortunately, the dog couldn't resist tipping over glasses and open beer containers to lap up the spills. On the rare occasions when his eyes were glossy he would bark ferociously and run at me. I would grab the end of my cloth bag to hold in the newspapers, jump the fence and race the young bull in the next pasture to the other side. I would make it across the field and jump over the opposite fence just in time. Then the bull would turn around and chase the dog that was right behind me.

It took two years of building up my list of customers to save enough money to buy a full-sized, brand new Columbia bike for my paper route.

When I was nine years old, I had to apply for a Social Security card to work full time at an apple orchard. I was using a 20-foot ladder and moving 40-pound boxes of apples around all day. The wage was $0.65 per hour at a time when I only got fifty cents for mowing a lawn or shovelling a driveway, so it was a big step up in income.

At that age, I thought it was funny that the one thing Brookfield Orchards withheld from my pay was Massachusetts Old Age Tax (MOAT). I recall that bills for meals in restaurants also had MOAT at the bottom back then. Sixty years later a Massachusetts State Senator said there was no such thing when I asked how to get back what I had paid in. After the 1950s it magically morphed into a sales tax and my MOAT money the state accrued suddenly disappeared (into the water trench around the politicians' retirement castles?).

On a farm, one learns to be creative by building or repairing things with whatever's available. Making a temporary coupling of oak to replace a broken steel part would allow the haying to get done before it rained. A hacksaw and a small sledgehammer can transform a piece of angle iron or pipe to reinforce a broken frame with a couple of bolts.

Invention was something that happened to get through every day. There was nothing special about using creativity to resolve a dilemma or two. It saved a lot of trips to the hardware store and time lost locating replacement parts.

The same approach would produce answers to questions never asked before to get to or return from the moon. On the space programmes, we never had adequate funding or time to order special widgets or tools. Often, prototypes were made with tape, rubber bands, shims, paper clips and 'C' clamps.

Chapter 3
The Pick of the Crop

An apple orchard was a great place to work. With a portable radio under a tree, we could sing along with the pop tunes of the day with music that actually had a melody, told a story and had understandable lyrics.

As long as I didn't get a sunburn at the beginning of the season, I always had a tan working in just shorts, socks and sneakers. We didn't know about sunblock, if it was available back then. The fragrant apple blossoms and the gentle breeze lifted your spirits when we would be throwing the cut applewood limbs on the flatbed truck from the heavy-duty winter pruning. Putting the old trucks in low, low gear, the steering wheel would only have to be adjusted when a bump was encountered or at the end of a row. Otherwise it would creep along and stay in the two ruts between the rows without a driver.

Like other fruitwoods, the cut apple limbs would burn with display of colours, so they could be sold at a premium for those who enjoy firewood with a personality.

In the spring as the blossoms began to fade, they were replaced by the pea- to marble-sized apples appearing in clusters. We'd be standing on rungs of a ladder all day thinning them out to give the chosen few mini apples on each branch a chance to reach full size at maturity. Thinning the crop would also reduce the weight on the limbs come harvest time. On hot, humid days we'd work a little faster in the sun to get back on the shady side of the tree. From time to time, we'd drink a little more water from the shared one-gallon cider jug of water laying in the grass.

There was one drawback when I started thinning apples the first year. For a while as I closed my eyes at night, all I could see was millions of tiny, green, wanna-be apples in the sunshine.

Were all the apples trying to say, "*Pick the others and let me stay?*"

In between pruning, thinning, mulching and picking, we learned to do the landscaping, painting and building of a new packing house with bunks upstairs for the temporary pickers from Canada and Jamaica.

I only had a couple of falls in twelve years' time at the orchard. They did have strict tongue in cheek rules for that.

First, "*You must holler when you start to fall so everyone can watch.*"

Secondly, "*You have to keep picking on the way down.*"

But most importantly, "*You can't bruise the fruit.*"

One time, I followed all the rules from what should have been a very secure ladder setting in the crotch of a pair of two-inch branches that split on me.

(Figure 7) Apple Tree

We used to kid new pickers about using a sky hook to anchor a ladder in a difficult setting. I should have tried one of them.

I ended upside down with my legs tangled in the ladder and my head just above ground level. The bucketful of apples on my chest had shifted off to the side and was hanging between my arm and rib cage. I hadn't lost any apples in the process, so I passed the acid test.

The orchard had the Morse brothers as year-round employees. Between the two of them they looked like an older composite of Bing Crosby and Norman Rockwell. The bespectacled, carefree Bill with his baseball cap was quiet, but happy. Grumpy Damon was known to give others grief from time to time. He always insisted that nobody could pick as fast as I did on piecework and not damage the apples.

There were some pickers who were brutal with the product when receiving a pay rate of 20 to 30 cents a bushel on piecework. If the stems were removed, the apples would not refrigerate well. If pieces of the branch were broken off with the apple that would eliminate the blossom for the next year's crop and the stick would puncture the apples in the chest picking bucket and box.

Damon would kneel down next to one of my boxes from time to time. Puffing on his pipe, he would remove one apple after another, carefully examining each one as he transferred it to another box. In between he'd keep looking at me up on my ladder, shaking his head. It was like a ritual with him, but he never indicated that he found a problem with any of the apples I had picked. He probably wanted to let me know he was watching me. I guess everyone needs a hobby.

Once he put a limit on the number of apples I was allowed to pick in a day at 100 bushels, so I slowed down a little and went home early. The next time he gave me a limit, I was told that I could only do 80 bushels that day on a prized variety of apples. I picked like crazy without a break and went home at noon after I'd reached my quota. He never gave me a restriction after that. It always amused me to bug him. I needed hobbies too.

In the fall, after the farmers in Nova Scotia finished their harvest in Canada, some would come down and pick apples in Massachusetts. They'd be put up for their stay in bunks upstairs in the new packing house. There was one young farmer, feeling his oats. He didn't know me but bet a day's pay that he could out-pick me on piecework. Not being shy about rising to a challenge, I said, *"Okay."* We worked hard all day without a break and he almost kept up with me. I felt bad for him but decided that I would have given him the 30 something US dollars

I'd earned if he had won. Apparently, he didn't realise I was a little taller with a broader wingspan. I could stretch six feet on both sides of my ladder, standing on one leg to balance and lean out. That meant I didn't need to move my ladder as often.

When something would come up that was difficult, Damon would ask me to do it. He'd say, "...*Because you understand that sort of thing*," while he puffed on his pipe. One day we came across an old Baldwin apple tree with a tall branch that hadn't been pruned but was loaded with apples. The branch extended well away from the tree with no place for a firm ladder setting. He had me go get the one 40-foot ladder we had. I straddled the ladder and balanced it vertically while I picked each apple and tossed it down to someone below. It was something I'd done many times before, but a gust of wind came up and I ended up falling headfirst toward the grass below. Fortunately, in gymnastics and wrestling you learn to tuck your chin down to your chest and try to land on your shoulders to break your fall. That move, and the tall grass cushioned the landing. My head was ringing for the next half hour, but I was okay after that.

Another adventure happened when I was painting the three-story packing house from a scaffold. The roof had a three-foot overhang which prevented the wide antique staging from rising all the way up to the peak. We put a stepladder on top of four wooden boxes on top of the swinging platform. I stood on the top step of the ladder while the owner's son, Tony was on the roof. He held the end of the rope tied around my waist while I stretched to finish painting the trim underneath the overhang. Back in the days when I was an indestructible teen, I 'knew' I could do anything and didn't consider things like that dangerous. That was 20 years before OSHA was created to make funny rules for worker safety when they didn't understand what was involved in the jobs at hand.

My brother Ron was two years younger than I but was three years behind me in school. Because I was slightly closer in age to my brother Jerry, Ron always seemed much younger. Oddly enough, I had never worked with him in the apple orchard. When Ron was complaining he couldn't make money on piecework above the hourly rate, I said, "*Why don't you pick with me today?*"

We went out and set up out ladders in the trees. I kept encouraging him to pick up the pace. He didn't make much above the day rate, but at least it was a start. Jerry did much better on piecework than Ron. That and eating pasta were the two things Jerry could almost keep up with me on.

Chapter 4
Siblings

When I went looking for a group photo, it seemed we were never all together at the same time. From left to right is Dad, Ron, Tim, Sue, Jerry and Russ about 1959. Mum took the picture. The sibling age spread was 17 years.

We all played musical instruments. My sister, Sue, Ron, our mother and I had varying degrees of artistic talent. Ron wanted to become an artist.

(Figure 8) Dad and Parker Kids

Unfortunately, his three older brothers (Russ, Jerry and I) convinced him there were too many starving artists in the world. Ron went to Northeastern University in Boston, MA under their five-year work/study programme to pay for his education. He went into business after college and hated it. He did end up in West Paris, but it wasn't on the west bank. It was in Paris, Maine instead of France. He kept heading north until they didn't have building codes.

After building a cabin for himself, Ron assembled a combination tool shed and outhouse. Years later, he's finally using a little electricity from solar panels. He draws water from a stream that is part of the same aquifer that Poland Springs uses. Now that he's retired, he finally has time to devote to his artwork and sculpting.

My sister, Sue, didn't show up until 12 years after I did, so I wasn't around much when she was growing up. Sue received her degree in education at what was Worcester State College in Massachusetts. Later, they changed the name to Worcester State University.

After starting her family, Sue did substitute teaching for a school year with four-year-olds until she could land a full-time teaching position. She spent 14 years teaching the second grade in Appleton, Wisconsin. Then she taught the third grade for another ten years after that. I can't imagine having enough patience to deal with munchkin issues for that long.

When I lived in Minnesota, a few people could tell I was from New England where they still speak the King's English because my accent had a hint of the Kennedy Clan's Boston Irish brogue. They also talk a different way out in Wisconsin. Sue had a number of funny stories about misunderstandings in classroom discussions with her students due to differences in dialects and nomenclature. In Minnesota and Wisconsin, sneakers or athletic shoes were called either tennies or tenny bumpers. The title of my first mystery was **WISPA** instead of whisper. In Massachusetts, it's also spelled and pronounced 'wispah'. What's also weird is that Cuba is pronounced Cuber in New England.

Chapter 5
Odd Jobs

I probably worked a little harder than most kids my age to keep jobs outside the farm after school and on school breaks. I learned how to grow and pick apples, trim hedges, as well as painting houses and barns. During high school and college breaks, I made moulds for pouring steel in foundries and processed raw wool to make yarn. I finished sheet metal for waterproof cases. I paved roads on construction. I lowered railroad track to let double-decker freight cars fit beneath highway over-passes.

I took any work I could find to make a buck. I never found anything that I couldn't do at least as well as the other employees. Besides picking apples on piecework and the tips working at a restaurant, my highest pay in high school was from working on railroad construction for $7.50 an hour.

Chapter 6
Woollen Mill/Sweat Shop

On the graveyard shift from 10 PM to 6 AM for a summer at Barre Wool Combing Company, I started tending a card machine (Fig. 9) that combed all the fibres to head in the same direction.

(Figure 9) Wool Carding Machine

At the front end, the wool was gathered into a large yarn called a sliver which was wound by a rotating head into a four-foot-tall cylinder. Maybe it was the lanolin in the freshly washed wool, but the smell always reminded me of freshly baked bread. When full, the container would be doffed (top layer of wool tucked inside the canister) and replaced. The cans would be then sent to the Spinning Department across the street to be twisted into tighter yarns.

Next, I was assigned to fill in on the wool washing operation. When the rinsed wool would jam up the gears on the open wire conveyer belt in the heated drier, I'd have to try to pull the snag out with a long metal rod with a hook on the end. If that didn't work, I'd have to duck walk beneath the chain link belt into the 140-degree Fahrenheit oven, holding my breath while I pulled the wool loose.

If I thought that was bad, then I was assigned to spread the wool in incoming bins upstairs. The next floor above is where they would start to take apart the bales of wool from places like Australia, New Zealand and Scotland. The bales were hard as a rock and seemed to consist of mostly briars and sheep manure. I assumed they bought it by the pound, so there was no incentive to ship a clean product. The four or five-inch-thick square chunks would be thrown on a conveyer that fed a trap door in the floor at the top of my bin. Then it would rain down on me, so I could build a 'dike' at the end of the bin to prevent the wool from spilling out into the aisle. I would continue to break up the 'slices' of the wool bale and spread it around the rest of the bin until it filled the 20 feet height to the top. At that point, I would climb out the hole and go down to start filling the next bin. Next a forklift with two large platens with huge 'spikes' would grab huge chunks from the full bin (like 'Jaws', the great white shark) to feed the chutes for the wool washing machine below that floor.

It wasn't long before I noticed the wool was coming down the trap door at a faster rate. As the bin filled, I heard the short foreman named Rosco above me say, "*Let's see just how fast he can spread the wool.*" When I poked my head up through the hole, I saw they had already added two more conveyors and were moving a fourth into position to feed my portal. Not seeing the humour in this, I grabbed Rosco's leg and pulled him down into the smelly bin. I was mad, so I hopped out of the hole and went for a long break before I punched out my timecard and went home. The next day, I was reassigned to the dye works.

Apparently, they were happy with my work, because I was the only summer employee to be called in on weekends at overtime rates. If I didn't need the money to pay for college, I might have thought twice about it. There were drains from the wool washing machines in the floor which were four feet deep and four feet wide trenches covered with heavy steel plates. A few of the plates could be lifted for removal. I would get in the trench in boots with a long metal bar that had a blade from a hoe welded on the end to loosen up clogs and build-ups of sheep manure in the corners of trench turns. The rest of the way I would have to waddle beneath the remaining plates. Did I mention how smelly sheep manure in a hot rinse water is?

On the third shift, I was paid a premium of five cents an hour. The weekend rate for overtime was a pay increase of fifty percent per hour, so it was a healthy bonus, even if I had to pay dues to the Textile Workers' Union. I wondered why the workers would stay in the union since the mill was the last of the sweatshops in the area, and the working conditions were deplorable. None of the regular employees had a full set of fingers and toes. Some workers had their prison numbers tattooed on their arms from the Nazi concentration camps.

After working the night shift at the woollen mill that summer, my day on the Boston and Albany Railroad ran from 7:30 AM to 3 PM out of the East Brookfield, MA train station. On weekends, I bussed in a restored colonial restaurant called the Salem Cross Inn which is located in West Brookfield.

Chapter 7
Restaurant

There were four Salem Brothers who owned trucking and warehouse companies, among other enterprises. When one of the brothers bought an abandoned house in the western end of the area that was once called Podunk by the Native Americans, they decided to convert it to a restaurant (Fig. 10).

Podunk made the national news when it supplied the Christmas tree for the Rockefeller Center in New York City.

(Figure 10) Salem Cross Inn

I seem to recall the announcer saying the huge 75 to 80-foot-high tree was, "*From a small town with the unbelievable name of Podunk.*" It was my understanding that Podunk was an Indian name, but I've seen where Podunk in American English describes "*a tiny, out of the way fictitious town*".

The towns of the Brookfields (including East, North and West Brookfield), and the Warrens were part of the Quaboag Plantation (established by land grants from the King of England) in the early days of the settling of the Massachusetts Bay Colony.

The Salems bought several run-down homes from the colonial era in the surrounding towns to salvage such things as mantles, wide chestnut boards plus gunstock and hand-hewn beams to rebuild the inn and refinish the adjoining barn.

I helped with the carpentry and masonry restoration work on the large taproom with the walk-in hearth downstairs used for roasting a side of beef with a roasting Jack from the 1700s. The weighted assembly in the roasting jack resembled the wind-up mechanism in a grandfather clock. It would rotate a side of beef over an open fire that was usually prepared for Drovers' Roasts, sleigh rides or hayride events.

The Salem Cross Inn name of the restaurant was derived from the family name and the witch marks (X) on the door that dated back to colonial times (1600s). The 'X' marks were etched over a doorway to keep the witches away.

A spring runs under the basement floor in a hidden enclosure to have fresh water available in case of a prolonged Indian siege.

Wearing a tie, dress shirt and red coat was challenging at times when trying to cover three floors at the same time. I had gone shopping at a shoe sale at Florsheim's at Washington's Crossing in Boston. Needing a size 12 with an EEE width, they were one of the few stores I could find shoes wide enough to fit my big feet. My father-in-law decided to tag along. He ended up buying identical wing tipped shoes, but in a size 11EEE.

Somehow, I ended up wearing his brand-new shoes at the restaurant the next day on Mothers' Day. Needless to say, my feet were killing me and covered with blisters when he finally showed up with my shoes at mid-afternoon. Before his arrival, I couldn't imagine how a pair of shoes could possibly be so uncomfortable.

He said, "I walked out your shoes and almost fell on the church steps this morning."

He did thank me later for breaking in his new shoes though.

Traffic of diners out for a Sunday afternoon drive was much heavier in the summer months. We had many high school and college girls filling in to wait on tables. Because I had a chance to train the new waitresses from the start, they would clean the plates to neatly stack the large oval trays. That way they could get three times as much on a single load as a few of the former hash house queens did.

One limitation for me as a busboy was that blue-nosed Massachusetts laws required an alcohol server to be at least 21 years old. I served drinks for the younger waitresses at their assigned tables for several years before someone who knew me well questioned it. Up to that point, if someone said, "*I didn't know you were over 21 Tim.*"

I responded with, "*Tim's my younger brother.*"

No one ever mentioned the fact that the under-aged waitresses and I removed all the glasses and bottles with liquor in them to clear the tables after. It seemed like a dumb rule to me, but I had to wait several months before I could work behind the bar or carry cocktails again.

One-night, people from the Mary Lane Hospital in the next town were having a Christmas party at the Inn. The band started playing so I was dancing with a waitress next to the lobster tank in a back room while we were waiting to clear the dinner dishes. A doctor poked his head in the door looking for a restroom and saw us. He decided to drag us out to the dance floor to perform for the group.

It happened that Chubby Checker's song 'The Twist' was the new dance rage at the time and our rendition was met with enthusiasm. My lithe partner, Marilee, was into gymnastics and only weighed a tad over 100 pounds. After a few numbers of throwing her between my legs and over my head between swinging her around, we were rewarded with resounding applause and a tip of $50 each. For a student who couldn't afford to purchase all the reference engineering and chemistry textbooks I needed for classes, that meant a lot. After that, they didn't have to ask us twice to perform for other groups.

On another occasion, I recall running through the main dining room with a heavily loaded, large tray in each hand that I had to hold next to the ceiling to weave through the crowd. In the middle of the main dining room there was an exceptionally attractive woman in a low-cut, white sheath dress with her hair done up in an elegant French twist. As I zoomed past her table, she had a forkful of whipped potato covered with gravy halfway to her mouth when it plopped down her cleavage.

As soon as I dropped the trays off in the kitchen, I returned with a water glass and extra napkins. After apologising profusely, I offered to pay for the dry-cleaning bill. She insisted that it wasn't my fault. She just claimed to be nervous with me weaving between all those people that fast.

One-day Dick Salem called me into his office and asked me to sit down. He proceeded to make out a check. He said, *"Now let me see, what can this be for? Oh, I know – books."*

I had never received a bonus before, so I was surprised. It was at a time when I was skipping meals, trying to make it through finals with a zero balance in my savings account, so it was really appreciated. I never told anyone about that because I suspected that nobody else got one.

Many years later Henry, another one of the original Salem brothers, was introducing me to his son David, who was much younger than I. David said, *"You're Tim Parker? You're practically a legend around here!"*

Chapter 8
Steel Foundry

Working at a now defunct foundry, I moulded cores for large pouring steel plumbing fittings (fig. 11). With so much carbon black (coke dust), my work clothes were too dirty to throw in the washer when I got home. Instead I'd stop at a lake, soap up my clothes and swim out to the raft and back so they were slightly cleaner, but wet.

(Figure 11) Pouring Steel

I worked beside a young Polish guy, who didn't speak much English. He was trying to earn enough money to bring his wife and kids over to the United States. Every day, I'd ask my mother another word or two in Polish, so I could tell him in both languages.

In between I would pantomime words and say the appropriate English word to him. One day when I was dancing around the core room, the general manager came in. I explained I was showing the guy the word 'dance' to increase his English vocabulary. After scratching his head for a minute, he decided it was a good idea, but added, *"Don't get hurt."*

Unfortunately, I couldn't have much of a social life. I would sleep through too many dates when I worked multiple jobs at the same time. When I'd asked my mother why she didn't wake me for a date, she'd say, *"You just looked like you needed the rest."* She was probably right, but I never got the chance to really get to know one particularly gorgeous girl better, a great tennis player and seemed to be just my type. After a half dozen dates I'd stood her up by sleeping late, too many times.

Chapter 9
Working on the Railroad

My first day on the railroad replacing wooden ties involved standing on one leg all day tamping crushed granite under the newly replaced railroad ties with an English garden fork. Even though I had to keep switching legs, I wasn't about to let the regular employees outlast me. Many of them were at least as old as my dad after all. It didn't occur to me that these guys had been doing flamingo and heron waterfowl imitations by balancing on one leg for years.

The railroad had a machine the size of a locomotive enveloped with a belt like a gigantic chain saw.

(Figure 12) Railroad Construction

Wrapping under the rails and ties, the huge belt with long teeth would dig under the rails, sift out the dirt and replace the crushed stone to lower the track. That way the double decker freight cars could fit under the highway over passes.

When ledge, massive boulders or old concrete foundations were encountered under the track, I seem to be the one selected to go underneath the machine with a jackhammer that was as big as I was.

I stretched out too many wristbands on my self-winding Timex watch that summer from all the vibrations. The television ads with John Cameron Swayze at the time claimed Timex was the watch that, "*Takes a licking, but keeps on ticking.*" While that may be true, their wristbands kept failing from the intense vibrations.

Once the track was lowered, a huge front-end loader would realign the rails except for beneath the underpasses. There, the crews had to buddy up on crowbars to finish lining up the track manually. It so happened that there were a couple of college football players on the other crews. Because any pair of the three of us would usually bend the steel crowbars, we were each only allowed to team up with a regular railroad worker.

To remove damaged or old, split wooden ties, a couple of guys would loosen them up with crowbars after the spikes were pulled. Then two or three pairs of other workers with ice tongs would pull the old ties out from under the rails. Usually we had to rush to get the ties replaced and spiked before the next train was scheduled to come roaring down the track.

At all these functions, we'd develop a rhythm that seemed to be choreographed. I don't recall anyone singing, "*I've been working on the railroad,*" though.

One day we were shorthanded to replace ties from under double and triple tracks. That meant more trains, shorter intervals between them and much longer ties. Before I knew it, we had one man with a crowbar. I was paired with a guy on the steel tongs who looked like John Henry. His biceps were the size of my thighs. He kept yanking out ties and smiling all day with no apparent effort on his part. Meanwhile my back felt like a piece of limp spaghetti.

At the end of the summer Andy, the foreman, came up to me to say, "*Let me know if you ever need a job again.*" I was surprised. Even though I always tried to do my best, Andy seemed to imply that my efforts were something special.

Chapter 10
Shipping and Receiving

On the next school break I found myself working in shipping and receiving at Brookfield Athletic Shoe Company with a former Marine who had been a boxer in the service. As soon as I arrived, Art started complaining that the kids who showed up didn't know what work was and he had to push them all the time to get anything done at all.

If that was a challenge, he didn't need to say another word to encourage me. Art was at the end of the roller conveyor unloading boxes while I walked back and forth in the trailer truck to load the conveyor. Even though I had to walk further as I approached the front of the trailer, I had the conveyor fully loaded with boxes because he couldn't keep up. He flashed a sheepish grin and doffed his tam cap to bow with a flourish in acknowledgement (Fig. 13 Loading Dock).

We got along fine after that except for an outside bell on the shipping dock that clanged when the telephone rang loud enough so we could hear it. If I happened to be within reach, I needed to be ready to block any punches he would throw when the bell sounded. You just can't trust former boxers.

One time there was an order mix-up and we spent hours transferring skates from Sear's boxes to J. C. Penny's. I was amazed to learn that the same exact skates at that time would go into boxes labelled, Sears, Penny's, Montgomery Ward's, etc.

(Figure 13) Loading Dock

One problem I ran into was that the company dump truck gas gauge didn't work. Usually you didn't know who used it last or how much (if any) gas was in the tank. After being assured there was "*probably enough gas*", I took the truck to the landfill. When I tipped the body back, the engine died and wouldn't restart. Even though there was no smoke in the area where I was dumping, the load ignited. The wooden truck body had been consumed by the fire before it could be extinguished by the local fire department.

When it was too late, a guy on the scene said, "*Why didn't you use the battery to move the truck away from the fire?*" It didn't even occur to me that the battery would have been strong enough to do that. I guess you learn something new every day. If it really worked, that doesn't explain why the firemen and the police at the scene didn't try it though. When I returned to the factory, the manager said not to worry about it because it was covered by insurance.

At each of those traditional jobs, I learned a lot that would eventually be useful in putting a man on the moon. It's possible I thought a little more about what I was doing than the average worker and how it could be done better or faster.

Chapter 11
School

Putting in all those hours working on and off the farm during the school year, I didn't have enough time to do a lot of homework. Fortunately, I could figure out things like math and explain concepts while I showed classmates how to do the homework during breaks in the school day. I was usually second or third in the class grade ratings, which was pretty good for a guy who rarely had time to complete the school assignments. I did end up speaking at graduation and was the recipient of four small local scholarships.

One teacher I had in high school for general science, chemistry and physics was a Mr George Dahlquist. He had a lot of pet expressions to maintain the class' attention and order. One was, *"No sideshows, come into the main tent."* I learned a lot from him. He also would say, *"The three rules of learning are repetition, repetition and repetition. Which is the most important? The third one."*

He convinced me to become a scientist, but at the time I let him down. He selected me for extra assignments which were well beyond what the rest of my classmates were doing. I felt it wasn't fair that he expected me to do all the additional work he was giving me. I resisted keeping up with the expanded workload because I didn't even have time to do the rest of my homework assignments for my other classes. I was just too tired from working after school, weekends, on school breaks and during vacations.

Mr D was serious about trying to instil a strong sense of intense curiosity and a hunger to learn in his students. In my observations from an experiment distilling water, I wrote in my notebook, *"Distilled water is colorless, odorless and tastes like rubber hose,"* (that I used in the experiment). I thought it was factual and funny, but he seemed disappointed in me for not treating the work more seriously.

Not too many years later I heard George Dahlquist had passed away at the young age of 42. I suspect that was only about a dozen years after I had him as a teacher. I'm sure he inspired many others in that short of a time span. I hope at least some of them came back to let him know how much he meant to them. I never returned to tell him what I had accomplished in my first decade as an engineer, but he probably would have guessed that.

In the lower grades, I read everything I could get my hands on, from contemporary novels to the classics. I took high school English literature tests from memory, because I was not inclined to take the time to read the same books again years later. I also learned more about English composition in Latin and French classes.

At the beginning of each English class, I would be the first to volunteer what I could remember about the novels I had read years before, so Mrs Murphy wouldn't call on me later in the period. She said I was given extra credit because of my contributions to the classroom discussions.

I did miss most of my childhood. Living a mile and a half from the centre of town and three miles from the new high school, I didn't have time for close friends. Scouting was fun, and I did get to camp out once at a Boy Scout jamboree with kids my age. I was good at baseball but found it boring. For me, high school sports were limited to a smattering of gymnastics and wrestling in physical education classes and participating on the track and basketball teams.

Naturally it was important for me to go to school to earn an income to support my future family better than my parents did theirs. Engineering had the highest average starting income for a bachelor's degree level during the time I was in high school. Chemical engineering was at the top of the income list. Selection of chemical engineering was an easy choice as a career for someone with a natural ability in math and science and no real preference.

Speaking of preference, the new high school guidance counsellor had us take a Kuder Preference Test. The first time the results claimed that I had no preference for a career field. I was the only one in a class of fifty who had to retake the test. The second time it said there was a toss-up between becoming an artist, musician or a hairdresser (?). My immediate response to that was, "*none of the above*," without any further deliberation.

Later when I got to college, I would throw the hammer and discus, but I could never get the techniques down to excel at the shot put or javelin. On the wrestling team, the cut off was 177 pounds below unlimited. One guy who was my size got down to the 167-pound weight class and he became much faster then. After starving myself for a couple of months, I couldn't get below 200 pounds, but I was still wrestling guys that weighed as much as 300 pounds. I was a lot faster but couldn't push them off if they got on top of me.

Since a couple of guys from my hometown were on the swimming team, I went to try out. The coach looked at my wide hands and feet and said, "*I've been waiting for years for a guy with paddles.*" He asked if I'd be interested in going out for the diving team too, so I gave it shot. Coach Rogers kept telling me, "*You need to come down closer to the board to achieve better elevation.*" That seemed to be happening until I took a bunch of skin off my stomach and nose by getting overly friendly with the end of diving board.

I also couldn't float well because of a large bone structure and muscle tone. That resulted in too much drag from riding low in the water on the crawl and the backstroke. My understanding is that swimming uses different muscles or at least uses muscles differently, so it's not good cross training for other sports. I also was not very good on the turns. After that I only competed in fraternity swim meets.

There was no time for real classmate contact in band, glee club or class plays in high school because I'd be coming from a part-time job or running off to another one after. The same was true for the ski and chess clubs. Water skiing was something you did when you could hitch a tow on a boat while waiting for it to snow again because skiing on snow was much more exciting. Racing downhill on skis at breakneck speeds with the wind and snow biting your cheeks was invigorating. The panoramic views of the hills and valleys on the horizon was one of the few pleasures I made time for.

Chapter 12
Bullies

If I'd been slightly more studious and smaller in stature, I might have been called a nerd and bullied. Back then, nerd wasn't in anyone's vocabulary, we were just ignored. The one time I was confronted by a bully in high school was by a kid who was a few inches taller than I was. It was hard to estimate his size because of his motorcycle boots with thick heels and his Elvis style hairdo. The boots and leather jacket both were adorned with shiny chains for some reason. He looked like he'd escaped from one of the gangs in the 'West Side Story'. His typical dress was kind of silly and out of place in a small Massachusetts farming community of 5,000 people.

In the boys' restroom, he tried to pick a fight with me by shoving me into a wall and ripping off my shirt pocket. I don't think he needed a reason. Naturally I retaliated by returning the shove while ripping his shirt. He looked like he was in total shock. I suspect nobody had ever stood up to him. Before anything else could happen, the principal came in and got between us. He was almost six feet tall with a crewcut but looked unsure about what to do next while looking up at the two of us. I suspect that he probably had problems with this troublemaker before.

In years down the road, I encountered problems with customers, suppliers, bosses and co-workers who tried to be bullies. One boss would be sweating bullets when he attempted to con a new sales manager at a major supplier for a lower price over the phone. He was one of the world's most negative thinkers. Whatever was suggested, he'd have a dozen reasons why we shouldn't do it. I'd have to come up with a lot more reasons why it should be done to convince him.

I had a customer who kept beating on me to drop my prices and would send defective goods to me (without authorisation) that were made by my competition. I was really surprised when he asked me to run his company in California for him a few years later. He probably figured I knew how to hold my ground.

I declined the offer, saying, *"Other than your highway traffic that doesn't move, Santa Anna winds, mud slides, forest fires, earthquakes, street gangs and boring weather, I can't think of a reason. Besides the cost of living is way too high out here."*

He said, *"What if money was no object?"*

I said, *"No thanks. California living is not the kind of lifestyle that I could tolerate."*

Chapter 13
Gemini, Earth Orbit

In 1964, I had an interesting start to my professional career at David Clark Company in Worcester, Massachusetts. It involved working on the cutting edge of materials and process engineering to meet demanding requirements for extreme environments on programmes with tight schedules. I found developing products for NASA, Army, Air Force, Navy, and Oak Ridge National Labs (NEA) to be exceptionally exciting. Most of these cutting-edge projects advanced the state-of-the-art in many different fields simultaneously.

All of this was pretty heady stuff for a country lad. Apparently, they found no skeletons in my closet when I was investigated for a security clearance. In keeping with the military policy of '*Don't Ask – Don't Tell*', outside of government circles, nobody asked what I was doing so I didn't have to tell.

One programme for the Navy was to make flame-resistant proximity suits (Fig. 14) for fighting fires on-board ships. To accomplish this, I compounded flame retardant adhesives on a rubber mill to laminate vacuum metalized reflective films and fire-resistant textiles. To make adhesives for these products, chunks of raw rubber the size of a lump of coal would be squeezed through a pair of opposing steel rollers to soften them.

(Figure 14) Navy Fire Proximity Suit

As the rubber warmed up from the friction generated and became more pliable, it would sick to itself like bread dough or taffy. After banding the rubber on one of the two steel rollers, the gap between the rolls would be tightened sufficiently to create a bead of rubber between the two rollers.

The other ingredients could be added slowly as they were incorporated into the bead of the rubber adhesive compound base. Most of the antioxidants, reinforcing agents, tackifiers, halogenated flame retardants, curing agents and stabilising additives consisted of powders or solid chunks. Adding liquids, such as plasticizers, required step wise, gradual addition to avoid turning the rubber band to mush.

Selective premixing of the fluids with the dry ingredients prior to addition helped maintain the integrity of the elastomer band on the roll.

To convince a glob of rubber adhesive base to stay on one side of a pair of opposing rubber mill rollers, cooling water flowing inside the opposite roller would keep it from transferring from the warmer roll. The compounding ingredients would be sequentially added to make it tacky, harden and resist flames.

Massachusetts has a requirement that a batch of rubber can't weigh more than the mill operator to prevent being pulled into the machine during mixing. To scale up the first large trial formulation in the plant I calculated the amounts of the ingredients necessary for a 200-pound batch for the production size rubber mill. I figured I was all set to train the mill guy on how to make it. When I arrived; I had an operator who only weighed about 140 pounds soaking wet. He could only watch as I went through the sequence to create the band of rubber and add the first few ingredients.

Because the rest of the additives make the formulation sticky and difficult to process, I had to return to the lab to split the remainder of the formulation into two smaller batches. After that I always asked, *"Who will be running the mill and how big is he or she?"*

When the mixing of adhesive stocks was completed on the mill, they were converted to a liquid form for coating by stripping off the material into a thin sheet by tightening the rollers together. Then it would be dissolved in a solvent blend, coated onto an aluminised reflective film and dried in an oven.

In production, the fabric would be wrapped around a heated steel roll while the adhesive coated film was pressed against the fabric by a rubber roller to assure full contact. To duplicate this effect in the lab, I would laminate the two layers together between a pair of heated platens with a high temperature resistant rubber pad to assure uniform pressure.

Ultimately, the final product passed the government test specification of withstanding two minutes exposure to radiant heat at 2,000°F without bursting into flame. At that time, the major competitors, such as the 3 M Company, American Optical and Mine Safety Appliances Company (MSA), couldn't pass the same test.

At first, the test fixture consisted of a carbon arc with a parabolic reflector, but it was later changed to a bank of quartz infrared radiant heaters.

I found a tightly woven fabric with a vacuum deposited double-faced aluminium metallization on a PET polyester film laminated with a flame-retardant adhesive worked best. Adding an opaque, water-resistant coating on the opposite side would last longer in the test when the radiant heaters couldn't be seen through the sample clamping frame aperture.

As with other projects and programmes there, I was proud that I accomplished the objective of this development task with no prior experience or guidelines on how to begin.

Following our nine-million-dollar production contract award by the Navy, I was extremely disappointed by the meagre raise I received in return after all that effort. It was then I started looking for another position to pay off medical bills and better support my family.

These textile composites were fabricated into on-board Navy firefighting proximity suits. The same technology was incorporated in the reflective fabric layers of the early US spacesuits (see astronaut suit fig. 4, page 24) with DuPont's new, flame-resistant type of 'Nylon®' (Nomex® aramid) and into bright metallic designer cloth for gowns, pocketbooks, shoes, belts and reflectors for auto windows.

Metalized films with non-woven fabric spacer layers also served as reflective insulation for the Apollo suit. Until the three astronauts were lost in the fire on the launchpad of Apollo 1 tests, plies of metallized PET polyester film (Mylar®) spaced with non-woven polyester fabric (Dacron®) were employed as a thermal barrier to reflect the heat of the sun and retain the body heat in the shade of space and on the lunar surface.

It was exciting to work with DuPont's latest aramid polymer fibres such as Nomex® and Kevlar®. Nomex® burns to a carbonaceous foam char when exposed to a direct flame.

Kevlar® has a higher strength to weight ratio than steel and is used in structural composite laminates for boats, aircraft and automobiles. The initial commercial product introduction was called Fiber B to replace steel belts on radial tires that would eventually fail by 'sawing' their way through the tires with the flexure of the tire sidewalls.

We were working with a much finer fibre version that had a lab name of PRD 49 (from Product Research and Development at DuPont). Kevlar laminates are also used for small calibre bullet protection in the military plus police helmets and vests.

A couple of decades later I was asked by the Coating, Laminating and Metallizing Division of TAPPI (Technical Association of Pulp and Paper Industry) to present a paper at their annual meeting in Boston on how a company can keep up with technology and market needs to avoid obsolescence.

In my presentation, I pointed out that lightly metallized (40 percent light transmission) film was laminated to glass on homes, vehicles and architectural glass windows to reduce heat loss and air conditioning requirements.

This combination of semi-transparent metal on film will also accelerate heating in a microwave oven for popcorn, pizza and browning or crisping foods.

Larry Tighe and I received patents for selectively printed semi-conductive coatings on microware packaging materials which can heat different foods at predetermined rates so the whole meal can finish at the same time. He wrote the conductive coating part of the paper that I presented.

That means you can service four diverse industries with variations of the same technology. The semi-conductive inks consisted of an evolution with different technology to provide an improvement for controlled microware heating with packaging. Our paper was featured in the TAPPI monthly magazine and later selected as one of the best papers in their five-year anthology publication. We were rightfully proud of our accomplishments, especially when the competition couldn't duplicate them.

Essentially the same product with a static dissipative coating and a heat sealable layer was used for packaging sensitive electronics to shield them from stray electrostatic discharges (micro-lightening).

After the Apollo fire when the three astronauts perished in a systems test on the launch pad, the outer insulating layers were changed to Kapton® polyimide film spaced with woven Beta Fiberglas® scrim sized with Kel-F® CTFE halocarbon resin. This improved flame protection of the composite insulation in a pure oxygen environment and integrity of the fabric spacer layer.

Kapton® was another DuPont high performance product with resistance to high temperatures for flexible circuits and flammability.

Kel-F® CTFE resin from the 3M Company has the best resistance to flame in a pure oxygen environment, but other polymers have more performance versatility in other applications.

This came about because the heat cleaned Beta Fiberglas® fibres abraded against each other in flex tests and ended up as glass dust in the seams of the thermal insulation outer garments

(ITMGs). I flame tested a Kel-F® CTFE size coating on the woven glass mesh with favourable test results.

With an upcoming flight scheduled, I couldn't find a coating company to produce the sized product version soon enough. It so happened we had a new lab under construction at that time. I made a trough with a thick nylon plastic sheet and electrical conduit bars to immerse the fabric in a solution coating of the CTFE polymer and wipe off the excess resin formulation. After passing under a bank of heat lamps to dry the sized (coated) mesh, it was rewound onto a cardboard core with a hand crank.

The Plant Safety Group had a conniption about the set up, but the lab windows were left wide open and the fans were blowing in fresh air for ventilation. It was another case of last minute drama, but I was happy I could resolve the challenge in time.

A sufficient amount of fabric was treated for the additional tests and retrofit use on the next set of protective spacesuits designated for flight missions.

After that flight, we were able to locate a commercial coating company to make more material on subsequent orders for future missions.

It may seem hard to believe, but steel and aluminium will burn in pure oxygen. In flame tests conducted in a pure oxygen environment Teflon is one of the most flame-resistant resins. Kel F® plastic is slightly more flame proof in the pure oxygen environment the astronauts work in but has a lower service temperature.

The flammability of Kynar® poly vinyl difluoride plastic (PVDF) is halfway between Teflon® polytetrafluoroethylene (PTFE) and conventional hydrocarbons like the polyethylene (PE) used in bread wraps and cosmetic bottles.

Forest firefighters carry metallized films that reflect the heat for survival blankets. Emergency Medical Technicians use them for patients suffering from hypothermia.

Thinner, semi-transparent layers of metal deposited on PET polyester plastic films (like Mylar®) applied with clear adhesive to architectural and automotive glass control thermal exchange in recreational vehicles, cars and high-rise buildings. The same products also protect sensitive electronic components from getting zapped by micro-lightening (electrostatic discharges) in shipment and storage. In microwave packaging, the same metallized film browns pizza and potpies plus it makes popcorn heat up faster to improve the yield.

One of the problems in getting vendors to work with us was that the quantities of parts and materials we needed were not that large compared to most commercial applications. With many suppliers, we had to wave the flag and talk about hot dogs, motherhood, and apple pie to solicit help for the good old United States of America in producing the '*right stuff*' needed to meet the requirements dictated by a mission to land on the moon.

Other firms were patriotic and more than willing to help. The advertising value of saying their product went to the moon on Apollo or was used in space orbit didn't hurt either.

At that time, DuPont was experimenting with their Nomex® fire retardant 'nylon' fabric we ended up using in the spacesuits. In its experimental phase on Project Gemini, it was called 'H-Fiber'. Now it's employed for fire protection in applications such as oven mitts, clothing for race car drivers, camping bags and for airplane curtains, walls, carpets and seat covers. When exposed to flame, it foams to an insulating carbonaceous char. By using two layers of Nomex®, the lower layer supplies structural integrity while the outer foamed layer insulates it from the fire.

The Project Mercury spacesuits offered a backup atmosphere to the capsule life support system and for the initial launches into space beyond Earth's atmosphere.

The high altitude, full pressure flight suits used by the military fliers were adapted for use in Project Gemini as the sole protection outside the flight module and for cabin depressurisation protection.

The Gemini Program's objectives also included longer flights, orbital rendezvous and vehicle docking in preparation for the Apollo moon-landing mission.

DuPont had developed Kevlar® fibre for radial tires (named Fiber B) to replace the steel belts which would fail by sawing through the rubber as the tire sidewalls flexed over road undulations and irregularities.

Another version with finer filament sizes was introduced as PRD-49 (Product Research and Development #49). In addition to having a higher strength to weight ratio than steel, Kevlar® is flame resistant and is employed in bulletproof body armour, cut resistant gloves, structural composites for aircraft, and tank lining laminates for hydrofluoric acid (which dissolves glass fibres and tank linings).

DuPont also developed a high heat resistant polyimide film called Kapton® (originally named H-Film) that when vacuum metalized, would serve as the outer heat reflective thermal insulation layers on the suits and modules. Known for resistance to molten solder baths and dielectric strength, flexible circuits are made from Kapton® today for use in appliance, automotive and electronic applications.

Both polyaramid materials were later incorporated into Apollo suits to solve design problems at higher temperatures where other materials wouldn't work.

Along the way in my career in research and development, I noticed that married friends without kids were being conscripted into the Army for service in the Vietnam War.

I had previously informed the Government Draft Board when I got married and had a child, but when I called the Draft Board, they still had me classified as a single ROTC student. They said that unless I got them a copy of my marriage licence and daughter's birth certificate, I was due to be drafted in a couple of weeks.

After sending them the paperwork, they said because of my Army ROTC training I would have preferred eligibility for the next 20 years, but I would go in as a sergeant.

Later my boss, Walter said he could have put me in for a special deferment because of the critical military and aerospace work I was doing. It took me by surprise that he thought my results in the lab were worth the extra effort on his part since I wasn't sure how to read him. My colleagues in the Research and Development Laboratory seemed to be afraid of him.

A co-worker told me a former Research and Development employee approached him and said, "*Walter, I was thinking about going back to school.*"

He immediately replied, "*That's fine. Clear out your desk and go to accounting to pick up your pay.*" End of discussion.

Walter was from the Ukraine had a strong Eastern European accent. When he dictated to his secretary Elaine, his 'W' would sound like the letter 'V'. Over a year went by before he noticed that his wiper seals were printed in reports as '*viper seals*'. In a loud voice as he made a hula gesture with his hand as he told her, "*No, no, no – Viper seal, as in Vavy like the ocean!*" That broke everyone up within earshot.

If he gave me grief on anything, I would mimic his pronunciation, but he didn't appear to notice it. He would eyeball a prototype I had just made and say, "*That does not look u-nee-form.*"

In my best imitation, I would say, "*Valter, that is too u-nee-form,*" with my co-workers snickering in the background.

Because his attitude could be interpreted as arrogance and his descriptions were easily misunderstood, we would hear side comments from military brass on plant tours, such as, "*He's either a genius or an idiot.*"

Back in the early 1960s, most people smoked, including when they were at work. A guy in the lab named Cliff smoked unfiltered cigarettes. He mostly did experimental electronics, vacuum testing and metalizing work which required using two hands.

To get a rise out of our secretary, he would straighten out a paper clip and insert it into a cigarette. When Elaine wandered by, she would watch the ash (supported by the metal wire) get longer and longer. Cliff would keep turning his head and blinking with the smoke getting in his eyes. He would end up with a full length of ash as her eyes kept getting bigger watching him while she was doing filing or whatever.

One day he got too cocky, and the cigarette burned down to his lips. With the wet paper sticking and the hot wire burning his lip, he was hopping around trying to flick it off. He never tried that again, but we had fun, even when it required working around the clock from time to time to meet deadlines.

A product we made for the astronauts to use with the suits after they splashed down in the ocean was a neck seal. It consisted of a tapered latex rubber circle with a neck hole mounted on a metal connector ring (the same as the helmet's ring) to mate with the suit ring. Basically, the fit on the neck was similar to that of a snug turtleneck sweater. When the capsule opened, it kept the suit from filling with water if sloshed with a wave or if the capsule upended at sea with the portal open.

One-day Walter tried on a neck seal but couldn't remove it. He had a larger than average neck size. A co-worker in the R and

D Lab named Sharon was a country gal from Athol, MA. She was two-thirds my size (but curvaceous and rugged). I have big hands that were strong from milking and picking apples on the farms all those years. If I wasn't around to help the other guys in the lab open stubborn chemical jars, Sharon would.

Walter asked Sharon for assistance in taking off the neck seal. He happened to be on the other side of a table. Sharon grabbed a hold on the neck ring and proceeded to drag Walter (who was built like a fireplug) across the table. Her final tug managed to remove it, but we thought his ears were going to rip off. Taking the neck seal in his hand, he said a meek, "*Thank you*," to Sharon. Then walked back to his office with his head a dark crimson colour.

My work included formulation, moulding and testing of high-performance rubber seals and gaskets for rockets and missiles. The compression moulding involved designing a mould, weighing out the amount of stock required and squeezing it out between a pair of mould halves to fill the mould cavity in a heated hydraulic press. I also helped develop and test headphones for avionics and ear protection.

Testing fabrics, rubbers, textiles, plastics and adhesives usually involved a tensile tester. In the early days, pairs of clamps would be tightened on each end of a sample to determine property variables such as tensile strength, tear resistance, peel/shear adhesion, compressive strength, elongation, etc.

The sample would be pulled or torn apart at different speeds by changing gears and weights on pendulum machines and recording the results from the dial.

It was time consuming to constantly make changes to the set ups every time a different material or test was run. Ultimately, people like the Instron Company in Canton, MA made testing equipment that was faster, more versatile and easier to change over from one type of test or material to another. Unfortunately, they were very expensive by comparison.

Testing and accelerated aging were done in ovens and environmental chambers. Special Tinius Olsen, Dillon & Thwing-Albert pendulum and 'hammer type' Izod Impact testers along with Elmendorf Tear testers determined tensile, dynamic tear and impact strength.

Some of these testers were developed for specific industries, such as paper, rubber, adhesives and textiles, in the prior century, but were adapted for newer materials.

Rubber and coated cloth diaphragms were evaluated for gas permeability, flex endurance, and bursting strength on other specialised equipment. MIT (Massachusetts Institute of Technology) came up with a flex fold endurance tester.

I found these assignments interesting and very exciting, although the pay could have been better for a newlywed with a baby girl at home. Unfortunately, we had separate health insurance policies. We discovered too late that a married policy would have been less expensive and would have covered the cost of a delivery with complications.

Who knew that the insurance company would withhold full maternity coverage? Another lesson learned. I had to earn extra money painting, working in a restaurant, wallpapering, pumping gas and picking apples on the side to pay all the medical bills.

Having made significant contributions to obtaining new business for the company, I felt the small raise I received in return meant that staying with the company wasn't in the best interest of my family. As much as I loved the work, I concluded that I should look for a better opportunity down the road.

President Eisenhower decided that sending military test pilots into space made the most sense to compete with the Russian threat of getting there first. Project Mercury scaled up from one astronaut per flight to two in Gemini (twins). Eventually, the programme morphed into Project Apollo for the Lunar Mission (three astronauts per flight) and the Space Shuttle (team of seven) for the Earth Orbit Space Lab Studies.

The programme presented a lot of challenges, but when Project Gemini phased down, I went to see if I could find a position with a higher salary.

It wasn't long before I had an offer at General Electric's Plastics Division. I agreed to report to work at General Electric Company in Pittsfield, MA, in a month's time. I couldn't afford to miss too many pay-cheques and pay my bills on time as well. After waiting two weeks before giving my notice, I crossed my fingers and told Walter I would be returning to school. He surprised me by wishing me good luck and saying I could return to the lab as soon as I was available again. I was able to work out my two weeks' notice.

Chapter 14
General Electric, Plastics Division

When I was hired at General Electric, my new boss, Bob, said that his budget was tight. He claimed that he couldn't come up with the salary I had asked for on his current budget. Instead he promised to give me performance reviews every six months for the first two years to catch me up.

Since there were no night schools in the area, I negotiated a flexible work schedule to take daytime classes at local universities. Naturally I didn't see any need to put this in writing. Why would he lie to me?

I started off working on chemical stabilising and scaling up the manufacturing process for a new, high temperature resistant engineering plastic at General Electric Company to be used in demanding commercial, consumer and industrial applications.

Inside of six months, Bob was transferred to another division and replaced by Tom. Of course, Tom said he couldn't be responsible for anything Bob had promised me.

As it turned out, there was a new chemical engineer from the Netherlands named Bernie (Dr Bernardus Jacob van Sorge) who had worked at DuPont Technical Fibers Division in Delaware for four years.

We were the only two engineers in our Research and Development Group. Naturally they put the two of us together in the same lab. The rest of the staff consisted of 38 chemists and laboratory technicians.

There is an old saying about the difference between a chemist and a chemical engineer. When presented with a problem, the chemist might come up with ten solutions and methodically try to produce a test tube of polymer with each approach. The engineer will sort out which two or three methods might be economically viable and will scale up at least a sufficient quantity to verify the theory. In our case, we needed to produce 500 pounds of heat-stabilized polymer to send to Japan for evaluation in our joint development effort of the two companies. Ultimately, Bernie and I were the only ones in our group to do that successfully.

We had a few chemists in our division who were exceptional. Many of the others knew their chemistry, but didn't know how to use that knowledge to get from step A to step D. Since most of them knew more about chemistry than I did, I would approach them and asked if I did such and such, would it get me from step A to step B and so on. Meanwhile, Bernie would talk to each of them to find out what had been tried in the past to see if there was anything that looked promising and what had been evaluated that didn't work.

At that time, GE decided they wanted to sell freight cars full of an 'engineering plastic' at a dollar per pound, even if it meant a sacrifice in performance. They didn't want to sell half the quantity of a superior product at two dollars per pound for the same net sales.

The result was to produce a polymer alloy (blend) with a lower cost resin that yielded intermediate properties between the two. GE did apply for patents on the improvements on the original resin, so the competition couldn't come back and eat our lunch with it.

Back to meeting Bernie. Upon introduction, I was astounded that communication with him was close to impossible. He wasn't fluent in English. Apparently, DuPont had left him off in a corner for four years to fend for himself. I couldn't imagine how that was possible. He was transferred from textile fibres to fabrics to carpet backings which reduced his area of responsibility with each step downward (i.e. he gradually became a *'specialist'*).

Bottom line is that every time he mumbled something I couldn't understand, I'd insist that he say it again, only louder until we both knew what he said in English. I'd do the same thing in reviewing his monthly reports before submission.

Bernie was on the short side (vertically challenged) with wire-rimmed glasses. When he got frustrated, his bald head would turn a beet red that was a stark contrast with the few wisps of white hair on the top of his mostly barren scalp. A little spittle would form in the corner of his mouth because he was trying to talk faster than he could get the words out in English. I'd wait for him to calm down and ask him to say that again s-l-o-w-l-y. Inside of six months he was thinking in English instead of his native Dutch, as well as speaking and writing our American version of the English language understandably.

Bernie was a somewhat unusual. He heard that the US Government was not going to make any more one-dollar paper certificates redeemable in silver after 1957. He started collecting the paper certificates and silver coins before the mint switched to copper composite coins in President Johnson's era and the Viet Nam War. His goal was to accumulate $1,000 to purchase a silver ingot to use as a paperweight on his desk.

Then he started taking flying lessons on weekends to obtain his pilot's licence. He'd also drive his big Oldsmobile sedan to visit old friends in Delaware as if he were flying down the highways. It would take him four hours for the five-hour trek. On the return of one trip, he missed his exit off the New York Thruway. Backing up to the exit ramp at a high rate of speed he slammed into a state patrol car. Flustered, he said, "I'm very sorry officer. I was upset because I just got a ticket for speeding and missed my turn off."

Getting back to my new boss, Tom, I was informed that he had his name on a half dozen patents. As I got to know him better, I couldn't believe they were his own work. Near the end of each month, Tom would be in my lab, looking over my shoulder and asking a million questions about what I was doing.

In a few months, I found he would be describing my projects as if they were solely the results of his efforts, but his summary reports were submitted for corporate review a few days before mine. From then on, I would make up things to tell him that were plausible, but slightly off the mark. Consequently, our reports never looked exactly the same after that.

Sometime much later, I was shocked when I read a GE marketing report. I thought that someone else in the company was working on a project identical to mine, but they came to entirely different conclusions. None of the graphs bore any resemblance to my plots and observations. Later I found out they rewrote my results and smoothed out the curves for presentation of product information to customers. Who knew they could do that?

Bernie and I assembled and ran a continuous, high-pressure reactor in the lab with stainless steel tubing. The goals were to improve the polymer heat stability and production output rate of the new, high performance plastic which was normally 'cooked' in a batch (kettle) process. Since he initiated the project and designed the reactor, I didn't have a problem that my name wasn't included on that patent application.

A thermoplastic polymer means the chemical building block units repeat in a chain that can be melted and fused together like wax. Meanwhile, the pilot plant was having trouble making a short-chained version (low molecular weight) for testing to obtain approval from the Food and Drug Administration (FDA), then the new plastic compound could be used in direct food contact. They made trial batch after batch and couldn't hit the target that would confirm that small particles of this polymer would not endanger livestock when ingested into their systems.

I 're-cooked' a standard production batch with a reaction by-product in a small lab bench sized reactor (like a pressure cooker with an external stirrer). It produced the desired result of reducing the average chain length with a significantly narrower molecular weight distribution. That way it could be fed by membrane osmosis to test animals to confirm there were no adverse effects for use in food packaging and processing. Once the lab results were verified, larger batches were made in production for the full-scale FDA testing.

When I wrote up the input for a patent application, General Electric claimed having the names of PhD chemists on it would increase the probability of having the patent approved. I was still scratching my head after I had to explain the entire process several times to these chemists, so their names could be on the patent instead of mine. Maybe that helped to justify their higher salaries? I never would learn how to understand company politics. Perhaps I don't work and play well with others after all (or with the right corporate people).

Working with the company in Japan, I started to make a grade of a high-performance fibre that was a spin-off (chemical cousin) of the plastic we were scaling up in production. The theory was that it took about ten years to produce a commercial product after process refinement and confirmation testing in the laboratory.

In the adjoining lab, there was a chemist named Bill Howe with a master's degree in chemistry. Because of his knowledge and dedication, he was affectionately known as Mr PPO (the chemical name of the original plastic was Poly Phenylene Oxide). He was kind of shunned because most of the chemists in our R&D group were PhDs, but I learned a lot of chemistry from him.

At times, Bill acted like one of the absent-minded professor types. It wasn't unusual for him to forget he was filling a water bath, so he'd be running down the hall in a T-shirt carrying a mop and bucket when it overflowed. One new secretary was surprised after being on board for a month to learn he wasn't a janitor.

Because it took so long for the equipment in the mini-plant to heat up to reaction temperature, Bill and I scheduled an all-night production trial run of a fibre grade. Since the reactor ran hotter than usual in this test, everyone else disappeared as more red lights than usual began flashing and the pressure gage readings were rising well beyond the normal operation range for the standard plastic reaction.

Everything went extremely well until a two-inch diameter pipe plugged during a transfer of the reaction batch to another vessel at two o'clock in the morning. Trying to open a drain valve, all we could get out was a small quantity of dark gel that looked like spaghetti embedded in firm molasses.

Bill said, *"There's nobody around at this hour. We'll have to take all the pipe fittings apart to clean them and then put them back together before the batch cools down and hardens."*

Standing next to a high-pressure air line, I said, *"Why don't I see if I can find enough reduction fittings in the machine shop to connect the air line to the transfer pipes, so we can blow out the plugged line?"*

Bill said, *"Let's try it. What have we got to lose?"*

I came back with a large box of plumbing parts. It took about a dozen of them to connect the small diameter air hose to the large pipe. Bill was in the next room looking into the open viewport on the large vat we were trying to transfer the batch to. I hollered at Bill to ask if he was ready. He yelled back, *"Let her rip!"*

There was a loud gurgling sound followed by a *Plow!* As I turned the corner Bill shouted, *"Hurray, it's free."* There stood Bill, covered with the 'spaghetti-molasses' mixture plastered all over his suit and tie. Until he removed his safety glasses, it was hard to see any bare spots on his face. He was just happy that we didn't have to take all the plumbing apart and throw out the whole batch. That's the kind of guy he was. To him it was more important to have successfully completed the project on time than to worry about cleaning himself up or the cost of replacing his wardrobe.

We took the next day off to get some sleep when we were done, only to find out upon our return that one of another division's union had filed a grievance against us. Apparently, we were supposed to wait for someone to come in on overtime to fix it, even though our division wasn't unionized.

The other six GE divisions in Pittsfield, MA belonged to unions that had contractual restrictions on the Plastics Division. It didn't matter that the equipment might have been ruined if we had waited to find union guys and get them to come in. We had no idea who they were or that we supposedly should have contacted them. We probably would have had to start another run all over again from scratch with no better chance of success anyway.

The head of our division called us in to say, *"Thanks for saving the batch, so it could be shipped to Japan on time for evaluation in our joint effort."* As an aside he added quietly, *"Next time, please don't get caught."*

I may have the record number of grievances turned in against me there since I usually couldn't get the union people scheduled in time to get my projects done. When a union complained because I installed a precision, direct current metering pump with a Teflon® membrane, they sent two master electricians with their apprentices to hook up the next one. I couldn't get anything accomplished in the lab with four of them in the way.

Then I had to show them how to hook it up. I was especially irked because the union electricians were making more money than I was. It took all of them twice as long as I did to install the first unit by myself. After that, I had to have outside union contractors come in if I wanted things finished sooner than the GE union guys could be scheduled to get there. We were the only non-union division of seven in Pittsfield, so why were they even involved? Not only that, when a union from another division went on strike, we had to wait to escort the women in our group through the picket lines to get into the building. Who knew? It was lousy contract negotiation management from what I could tell.

Friden calculator (Fig. 15) is an example of how much technology has changed in a relatively few years. They were the size of IBM Selectric typewriters. In 1965 we still used Friden mechanical calculators to derive standard deviations on our experiments (measure of data accuracy). If the thing jammed, you could lose up to a half hour of calculating time and need to start all over again.

(Figure 15) Friden Calculator

Imaging how thrilled we were when an electronic calculator was purchased in 1966 for $50,000. It was a big box, the size of a desk sitting on a desk. Punching in the numbers and seeing the answer show up immediately on a little two-inch-by-two-inch window was like magic. That huge unit didn't do anything more complicated than the credit card sized calculators of today, but we had a long, continuous queue of professionals standing in line, waiting for their turn to use it because it saved so much time.

Ten years later in 1976, a three inch by four-inch Texas Instrument Scientific Calculator was about an inch thick (not quite pocket sized) and cost over $400 but could perform many more functions.

I never learned how to type. To use the mainframe computer at GE in Schenectady, NY, it would take me over an hour to enter my data on little yellow perforated tapes. Then I'd feed the tapes over the telephone lines and get the processed data back in a fraction of a minute. It was so fast; I was discouraged because it took so long to make the yellow tapes in the first place.

To make things worse, the consistency of the data would also be rated with one, two or three asterisks with three being the worst. There was a technician named Mary who was a sweetheart and resembled a rosy-cheeked Mary Poppins. She needed extra money as a single parent. On occasion, she would enter the numbers on overtime for us. We had a clown at the corporate office on night shift who would swap the three-asterisk punch card for one that said the coarser equivalent of, "*You screwed up again Charlie.*" If the data left something to be desired for variability, Mary would turn scarlet when that printed out.

Overall, we had a great group and a lot of fun working there, but the new plant was being built in a much higher cost of living area (Selkirk) in upstate New York forty miles south of Albany. The financial incentives provided to those of us with offers to move were too low compared to the higher cost of living the area, so most of us left the company.

I was offered a position at Fairchild Semiconductor in Portland, Maine supervising row after row of women working under microscopes in clean room, white 'bunny suits' on tiny little widgets. I couldn't imagine how these workers maintained their sanity performing the same exacting functions day after day in their confined workspace. Talk about high stress jobs.

Unfortunately, this was before the harbour was fully cleaned up and renovated. We took a ride up to look over the neighbourhood. Because the area still looked like a slum, the wife said, *"We're not moving here!"*

With that decided, we opted to take the aerospace position I had been offered in Delaware instead.

Chapter 15
ILC, Apollo, Helmet and Cables – 1967

Following General Electric's Plastic Division plant relocation to upstate New York, I returned to the aerospace field on Project Apollo.

Moving to Delaware from New England was something of a cultural shock. Here I was starting to work on high technology materials, processes and applications again. In a dramatic contrast to what I normally experienced in Massachusetts, every day I encountered Amish horses and buggies filled with the *'plain people'* slowly flowing with the traffic on the main streets in the city of Dover, the state capital.

Mennonite farmers also lived in the area, but they drove pick-up trucks and tractors. They also used new-fangled things like zippers and snaps.

International Playtex and International Latex Companies (ILC) became involved supplying the military with parachutes, floatation devices and rafts during the war. The Government and Industrial Division eventually became known as ILC Dover.

Likewise, David Clark Co. in Worcester, MA (Division of Munsingwear/Penguin) made the transition from bras and girdles to supplying the military with parachutes and flight gear in World War II before venturing further into military and aerospace products.

The Apollo Program involved putting men on the moon and bringing them back safely. How does one begin to do that? The exact details of what the environments in space and on the lunar surface remained unknown at that point in time. This was especially true regarding the degree of danger from long-term exposure to cosmic radiation and frequency or size of micro-meteoroid impacts. The astronauts were puzzled by the little lights they were seeing in space, only to be later informed that they were the result of cosmic rays impinging on their eyeballs.

The construction contract to build spacesuits and accessories which would permit extra-vehicular activity (EVA) in space and on the lunar surface by the astronauts did not include funds for development. Each time an unforeseen problem or new requirement was encountered, a proposal needed to be generated and approved to obtain additional funding. It didn't matter that it hadn't been done before. We just had to come up with at least one viable solution in a timely manner for each challenge presented.

After being hired as a Reliability Engineer in Quality Control, I identified potential design flaws and recommended corrective actions. The first defect I encountered was the stress crazing of the plastic helmet around the holes drilled to mount the Feed Port and Emergency Oxygen Supply Assembly (Fig 16). We didn't know if this micro-stress cracking would ultimately become catastrophic whereupon the astronaut could lose his head in space or on the lunar surface.

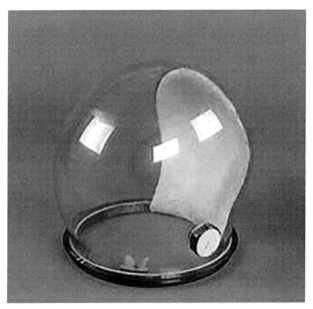

(Figure 16) Feed Port on Helmet

81

Working with General Electric, a supplier of clear Lexan® high impact polycarbonate (PC) resin used in the helmet, resulted in revised machining procedures to resolve the drilling issue.

Down the road, when I had the helmet stress tested with pure oxygen at overpressure through the equivalent of ten mission cycles, there was no sign of failure.

Many years later I was told by a colleague that my approach of sifting through all the layers of a company to find the one individual who could help me was unusual. That was always the approach I used and apparently, I was good at ferreting out the right technical experts at all the suppliers we dealt with.

Next the suit cable restraint systems had trouble passing the same ten-mission cycle requirement. If a man is inflated in a pressure suit, he'd look like the 'X' configuration in Leonardo da Vinci's sketch (Fig.17) without cable restraints.

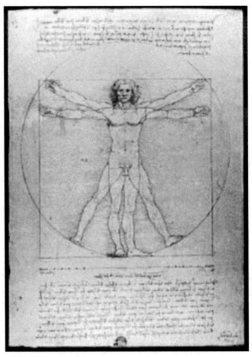

(Figure 17) Leonardo Sketch

Nylon® coated stainless steel rope control cables are used for marine and aircraft applications. In the Apollo suit, leverage for movement of the arms and legs and the ability to hold a position was provided by this type of cable. Small metal tubes lined with PTFE Teflon® tubing guide the coated wire ropes around curves. The friction between the coated cables and the fluorocarbon liner hold the astronauts' extremities in place. Unfortunately, the Nylon® over-coating would heat up with rapid cycling and it could be torn by the steel cable fibres as they abraded each other.

I contacted the wire rope manufacturer to determine our options. It seemed that the standard extrusion process for application of the Nylon® overcoat was called 'Tubed on' and resulted in little penetration of the resin into the wire cable fibre bundles to hold them in place. They asked what they should do about the existing purchase orders for coated cable. I said, "*Put them on hold since that approach didn't work.*"

When the Purchasing and Production Departments at ILC Dover found out I had tabled the cable order, they went ballistic. It was pointed out they had a contract to make a product defined by specification, whether it worked or not. Continuation of production with components that would need immediate replacement made no sense to me but acting responsibly without authority appeared to be frowned upon. Perhaps they figured that a suit with any kind of cables could be designated for '*training only*' until it was retrofitted after the problem was resolved.

In a few weeks' time, I had developed, and cycle tested two new configurations of cable for the equivalent of ten mission cycles. I hopped on a plane to Houston, Texas. Upon arrival at the Manned Flight Space Center, I obtained directions to find the appropriate NASA Project Engineers after clearing the reception area with a temporary visitor's badge. Approaching the two guys leaning back in their chairs with their feet up on their desks, I overheard them talking about the cable design. One said my company was… "*Beating a dead horse trying to fix the wire rope restraint system.*"

The other agreed completely and said, "*It will never work.*"

Introducing myself, I pulled out coils of both new cable designs and a detailed test report from my briefcase. I informed them we had successfully tested one new version of coated micro-line cables wound together and over-extruded with a pressured-on coating. This would translate part of the tension load to compression of the Nylon®, but would require a new end clamp design.

Then I informed them that wouldn't be necessary because application of the Nylon® at a higher process pressure (the technique called '*Pressured on*') to lock the wire rope fibres in place worked fine in the original suit design configuration.

I patiently answered all their questions and walked away knowing I didn't "*make friends and influence people*" by proving them wrong in my initial encounter.

Later in the programme, NASA wanted assurance that our crimping process of the copper swage over the Nylon stripped end of the cable would hold the stainless-steel strands uniformly to distribute the load. To do this we had to concoct two different acid etching solutions to examine both the copper swage and the stainless-steel cable separately. Inspection of the two components etched independently provided the confirmation of the load distribution requested.

Chapter 16
Problem Solving Approach

Like doctors, many scientists want to specialise in a specific area of their field. As the old saying goes, by concentrating on certain aspects of a single technology, specialists *"begin to know more and more about less and less"*.

Because I was generalist, if we didn't have an authority who was well versed in a given area of technical expertise, many problems ended up being assigned to me. That was because I always seemed to know a little about the subject involved. Of course, then I had to get up to speed in a hurry and fix *'it'*, whatever *'it'* was at the time. For me, I always saw that as a challenge, because I never learned how to think inside the box.

If I looked at a plastic process that wasn't working as it should, I would consider the fact that wax, metals, ice, glass, etc. all melt. Knowing how these materials are worked in the solid and molten/fluid forms could result in an easy solution that a plastics engineer would not normally contemplate. Incidentally, this was about time that plastic engineering finally became a major field of study at a few technical universities.

The same approach goes for paint, coatings, dyes, ink and food preparation. If you want a liquid solution, a dye can be dissolved in water or a solvent. Suspension of a pigment or particulate can become the first step in the manufacture of a cosmetic, auto polishing paste, turkey gravy or a latex paint.

Many otherwise brilliant people I've worked with through the years never looked to consider what other technologies have available to offer. Instead, they try to *'reinvent the wheel'* when other wheels already exist in the next laboratory or down the hall from where they are working.

Instead of developing a new approach from scratch, one should consider if available technology in another field can be easily altered to accomplish the same purpose. Otherwise, do you really need a wheel? Or can wheels be put inside a track like a snowmobile or a bulldozer that would provide better traction on snow or mud?

It may sound silly, but someone else's design for a lawnmower can be patented if your modification provides a unique and useful function. A lawnmower that has a muffler with a vast improvement in noise reduction which doesn't disturb the neighbour's sleep on a Sunday morning can incorporate someone else's design configuration which is already patented.

Once I was a passenger on a flight sitting next to an aeronautical engineer who designed turbines for jet aircraft. He told me they hired this young whippersnapper straight from school who had the nerve to ask why they were using a particular weld material for the turbine vanes. The kid was informed that was what they had always done. When he asked how they were failing in the field he learned that they had never looked into that. When they did, it was determined that the welds employed were brittle at the cold temperatures encountered at commercial flight altitudes.

Concerned about the safety of the flight we were on, I immediately asked if the plane we were flying on used their engines. He assured me that retrofitting of all the engines with new rotors had just been completed. Needless to say, that was a relief.

That was about the time I found out that most mechanical engineers I worked with didn't know much about non-metallic materials. I soon learned that they didn't pay much attention to welding, heat treating and finishing metals either. So, my group also had to double check their drawings and process specifications for metal processing techniques as well.

Management soon realised I could identify potential design flaws and recommend fixes faster than the changes could be implemented. After being promoted to Project Engineer, I ended up as Supervisor of the Parts and Materials Engineering Group in Apollo Project Engineering. My group worked with innovative material manufacturing leaders in the United States such as Dow Corning, DuPont, The 3M Company, GE Silicones and Owens Corning Fiberglas® to solve each new application or requirement encountered.

John was a physicist in Project Engineering when I joined that group. He had gone to night school about nine years to get his degree while he was working full time and building a house for his wife and four daughters. Ultimately, he joined ILC Dover from Goodrich Corporation in Ohio who had been competitor for the Apollo suit and accessories contract with NASA. One thing that amazed me was his ability to sit on the other side of my desk and proof read a new specification we had to get released to the production floor in a hurry. Not only did he keep up with me, but he was reading it upside down.

Under the shadow of World War II and the Korean 'police action', NASA and the military still required use of only materials and equipment made in the United States to avoid shortages of goods from foreign sources in the event of future military conflicts.

We were unaware that the Russian spacecraft disintegrated upon re-entry because they lacked an ablative coating and the leading-edge blunt design configuration we were using. An ablative layer cools the surface as in burns off in the atmosphere.

Unfortunately, we needed titanium for our space programme and had to have a third party purchase the metal from the Russians.

One process chemical from Norway we used required special documentation to prove there wasn't a comparable domestic source. Canada had the same requirements for their government purchases, but I think they still enforce their in-country procurement laws up there.

Now our military and government agencies purchase weapons, tools, equipment and vehicles from foreign sources with US taxpayer money, even if it puts Americans out of work and the other countries won't buy American products.

In response to what was known as the Sputnik Crisis in 1958, under President Eisenhower's administration, Congress established the space programme to counter the perceived Russian threat. A security clearance of '*Secret*' was needed to work on the NASA Mercury and Gemini Space programmes at that time. When I re-entered the aerospace programme on Apollo, I was surprised that the NASA security level had been downgraded to '*Confidential*'.

I didn't think much about it until I was asked by another group in the company for help with a highly classified military problem. After I sat down and was introduced to everyone in a conference room, they showed me a part and wanted to know how they could fix it.

I asked, *"What is it?"*

They said, *"We can't tell you because you only have a confidential security clearance level now."*

I asked, *"What is it supposed to do?"*

They said, *"We can't tell you that."*

I asked, *"What is wrong with it?"*

They said, *"It failed and doesn't work."*

I asked, "What *environment was it exposed to?"*

They said, *"We can't tell you that either."*

I launched into a monolog and said, *"Okay. We're not getting anywhere with this 'discussion'. It looks like it is supposed to be this kind of 'widget', made out of 'this kind' of rubber, that's been exposed to 'this' environment. You should change to 'this other type' of elastomer, compounded with 'this class' of antioxidant and a curing agent of 'this' family."*

They scratched their collective heads while taking a bunch of notes. The project manager stood up and said, *"Thank you very much,"* as he shook my hand.

About a month later, one of the engineers came up to me. *"You solved our problem. We just completed the accelerated aging tests and the new part held up fine. Thanks again,"* he said as he gave me a pat on the back.

This time I was the one standing there scratching my head. I had no idea what I did for them because my original security clearance level had lapsed while I worked for General Electric's Plastics Division, I'm sure I could have been more helpful if they had supplied me with a few details. I was just glad I could be of assistance with so little input from them.

The downside of trying to be all things to all people as a generalist is keeping up with technology in so many fields that were evolving exponentially. Joining several associations kept me more than busy. SAMPE stood for the Society of Aerospace Materials and Process Engineers, the AMA was the American Management Association, AICHE was American Institute of Chemical Engineers, ACS was the American Chemical Society and ASQC meant American Society of Quality Control. Plastics, rubber, AIM, NAME, TAPPI, PSTC, plastics, design engineering, corrosion engineering and many other industries had separate organisations that I belonged to. Each had one or more monthly magazines that I subscribed to in order to stay abreast of the latest materials and problem-solving techniques.

In addition to presenting technical papers at meetings for these organisations, I had accumulated about ten NASA New Technology Reports (equivalent of a US Patent) on my aerospace work.

Chapter 17
Need for Humour

In a hectic environment with mission schedules and requirements constantly changing, it helped to have a warped sense of humour to avoid going crazy or developing an ulcer.

(Figure 18) Mercury Capsule

On Alan Shepard's Mercury MR-3 flight, he noticed a sign in the cramped module quarters (Fig. 18) left by Astronaut John Glenn that read, "*No handball playing in this area.*"

Waiting for lift-off of the rocket, he looked around and thought, "*All of this was built by the lowest bidder.*"

After waiting four hours on his back in a launch position, Shepard was growing impatient and said, "Why *don't you fix your little problem and light this candle?*" Later he realised that they were concerned for his safety and only wanted to make sure everything was working properly. The 1961 Freedom 7 flight on a Mercury-Redstone rocket made Shepard the first American in space. Much later, during the Apollo 14 lunar mission Alan hit a golf ball on the moon.

We had a hardware/connector supplier named Jim who loved to pull pranks. His company supplied the precision-machined pressure seal fittings to attach the helmets, gloves, boots and the backpack interconnects to the suits.

The factory and office area of the plant in Delaware was surrounded by an eight-foot-tall cyclone fence topped with barbed razor wire. One-time, Jim rented a hearse, pulled up to the guard shack and said he was there to pick up an employee who had passed away. He drove inside the fence without signing in and parked at the loading dock while we had our meeting.

Jim was a pilot and at times he would fly himself down from his company in Connecticut. Once he was running late to catch his commercial return flight out of Philadelphia, so he called his friends in the control tower. The plane had already taxied down the runway, but they turned it around and returned to the gate. As he boarded the flight, everyone wondered who this VIP was to deserve the special treatment.

On another trip, he dropped out of the clouds to get his bearings flying home. He found himself right in front of the bridge over the Hudson River. He claimed he cleared the top of it, but his passenger swore he went under it.

There was a NASA Project Engineer in Houston named Ralph who ran helmet crash tests using cadavers on rocket sleds. In his report, he said a helmet should be shaped like a human head to reduce injuries sustained by restricting the skull travel distance upon impact. He received an award for his conclusion that should have been intuitive without testing.

Because of Ralph's argumentative nature, he was told by his boss in a NASA design review meeting to sit down and shut up, so we could get work done. Then someone had the bright idea to write a Work Request Form (WRF – pronounced warf) to authorise a manned helmet impact test headfirst off the company water tower into the parking lot with Ralph as the test subject. After being signed off at the company and NASA Houston, the WRF was forwarded to NASA in Washington, DC for the final touch. With full approval, the test could have been run if Ralph was willing to participate.

Ralph's selected helmet shape worked for all the astronauts except for Air Force Colonel Frank Bormann (USAF). His head was too big, so he required a larger spherical shaped helmet. As Commander of Apollo 8 flight on Christmas Eve of 1968, he was on the first manned flight to circle the moon. Later he became the President of Eastern Airlines. The same helmet configuration was worn for the movie astronauts in 'Marooned' with Gregory Peck in 1969.

Running headlong into unplanned, last minute difficulties was the norm. Compared to other places I'd worked, there seemed to be more open and closet alcoholics than average who caved under the ongoing pressure to meet programme deadlines.

One guy with two young children was wiped out by a chicken truck while driving his VW Beetle home from a party. Not too long after, another lost a leg and vision in one eye after being extricated from his wrecked car. One engineer had a clean, organised desk but would reek of alcohol coming back from lunch. He always came in on time for work and took off like a shot at 5:00 PM. He wasn't in my group, so I assumed he was functioning well enough to keep his job.

I had an engineering student named Pete from the University of Delaware working for me one summer. He came up to me to ask what was next after he completed an assignment. I said, *"Follow me."*

He said, *"Where are we going?"*

I told him, "We are going to make a jam sandwich. First, I'll heat up the press while you get some uncured rubber stock from stores and five mil shims (0.005" = thickness of masking tape) from the model shop."

Pete opened a micrometre (thickness gauge), looked at the tiny gap for 5 mils and said, *"That doesn't even look like it's thick enough to be worth bothering with."*

For a mechanical engineering major who was accustomed to dealing with much thicker structural metals, I thought that was funny.

When he returned, I showed him how to stack the uncured rubber on a thick metal plate, place the shims around the edges and cover it with another plate. We put it in the press for a preheat and then 'jammed it together' at high pressure. He seemed a little surprised at the thin piece of rubber that came out, but he had already seen a number of operations by then that they don't teach in engineering school. Pete ultimately became Director of Manufacturing for ILC Dover.

About that time, Astronaut Walt Cunningham was giving a pep talk to the production people on the importance of their work in the programme. He said, *"If my suit sprang a leak on an EVA (*Extra Vehicular Activity = spacewalk*) or on the surface of the moon, it could ruin my whole day."*

I wrestled with the same thought as the designated Apollo Project Engineering Representative. I had to decide to: use as is, fix or replace non-conforming components on Discrepant Material Reports (DMRs) for the Materials Review Board (MRB). After too many sleepless nights, I concluded that the astronauts were at least as brave as I was. That meant the solution was simple. I only had to determine if I would be willing to fly on a mission with it in the original, repaired or replaced condition.

It's too bad I never got the chance to fly though. The one time I tried to don a suit to check out a problem, I couldn't fit. I held my breath and curled up in a ball to no avail. To reduce module space and payload weight in the earlier orbital flights, the selection process favoured shorter astronauts.

The suit had about 1,500 different materials. I carried all the part numbers and specifications around in my head because I had written most of them. In subsequent career positions, I made it a point to try not to fill my brain with numbers.

Building and fixing things always came easy for me. I thought I was about average at anything I attempted. I used to say, *"Anybody can do anything if they try hard enough."* Turns out I was partially right. The Apollo Project Engineering Manager told me, *"You are getting all the top priority projects because of your batting average."* When I considered his comment, I noticed many tasks for my group were reassignments that others couldn't do. I'd been too busy with the work in our group to notice what others were or weren't doing. Upon reflection, maybe it should be revised to, *"Anyone can do anything if they have the right instructions."*

I also recalled my high school principal saying, "*If you don't think you're good, no one else will.*" Or maybe I really was better than average. I was too busy to consider that. I figured if I continued to do my best, then I could demand the same performance level from others to get the job done. Meeting all the challenges and deadlines on an on-going basis was an invigorating experience.

Chapter 18
Problems-R-Us

Buzz Aldrin (nee – Edwin Eugene Aldrin, Jr.) was the second astronaut to walk on the moon after the Apollo 11 mission commander Neil Armstrong in July of 1969. Having served as an Air Force fighter pilot in the Korean War, Aldrin received a PhD in aeronautics and astronautics at MIT. He was selected for the earth orbit crew in 1966 on Gemini 12 in the NASA space programme with Jim Lovell. His five-hour EVA (spacewalk) was the longest up to that point. During that flight, he had to manually calculate the docking manoeuvres after the on-board radar failed.

The astronauts had major problems floating in space where they would use so much energy trying to perform tasks at zero gravity, they would become exhausted. To replicate working in space, Buzz developed improved techniques in a deep-water tank at Johnson Space Center underwater wearing a spacesuit with counterweights adjusted to maintain buoyancy.

Basically, the people in my group worked as freelance designers and problem solvers in addition to being responsible for documentation. Our typical assignments had short fuses for completion before the next mission schedule, so everything was a rush. Sequencing almost didn't matter because all the tasks had to be finished and documented well before the next flight.

Many times, we were writing the specifications, procedures and documents after we built prototypes, some of which became flight hardware. One example was when NASA planned to do a deep core drill on the moon. Up to that point, quarantining the astronauts after the initial moon shots showed no signs of bugs (creatures) that were brought back with them from the lunar surface. There was concern that some kind of fungus or organism might survive below the surface of the moon, however.

I had to come up with a protective cover garment that would shield them from bringing any 'alien hitchhikers' back to earth. It couldn't weigh anything or inhibit the astronauts' movements. To meet all the requirements, I specified a non-porous silicone rubber coated fabric 'overcoat' that was to be left on the moon when the core drilling was completed. No problem, just a lot of hustling for another unplanned programme addition.

On another occasion, the astronauts reported they couldn't throw switches and turn dials with the outer thermal gloves in the ITMG (cover garment) over the pressure gloves in the PGA (Pressure Garment Assembly). Flame protection without the insulated outer gloves needed to be provided in the event of a fire inside a module. One of the consulting chemists on loan from LTV Aerospace in Texas was named Joe Young, like the movies, but he didn't have a gorilla suit. We worked around the clock applying a fire-resistant, fluorinated elastomer (a Teflon like rubber) coating to the pressure gloves to have them ready for the upcoming mission. As we figured out how to accomplish that, the process needed to be fully documented. At times we couldn't seem to get enough sleep.

In my original group, I had a physicist also named Joe. We called him *Mr Wizard* because he resembled a character of that name on a kids' TV science show at the time. George was a biochemist known as *The Alchemist* of our group. Doing most of the formulations and compounding, I was *The Shit Mixer*, because I put things together that chemists told me would not work. That was a big step up from being a shit kicker on the farm where I just wanted to get the manure off my shoes before I went back into the house.

A former Goodrich industrial engineer assigned to me was meticulous in his documentation assignments, but he had one annoying habit. When we were in the process of completing a project that we had to really scramble to finish on time, Lou would say*, "That reminds me of a problem that came up twenty years ago we solved by…"* As a result, at the start of a new task I would ask Lou, *"Does this smell, taste, feel or look like anything you have done before?"* There were occasions when he would give us a jump start on meeting a new requirement with the use of prior solutions in other applications. The trouble with many professional problem-solvers is they don't draw from their entire background and experience. I spent a lifetime learning and used every bit of both to solve new problems.

During high school, I worked nights in an antiquated woollen mill that was one of the last sweatshops. Because of the exposed leather shared belt drives on the machinery, almost none of the permanent workers had a full set of digits. What I learned about wool processing helped my understanding of processing space age fibres and textiles.

I was thrilled when we hired five recently graduated textile engineers. Finally, I thought we would be getting help in that area. One majored in textile design (fashion). Another we razzed because he specialised in knitting. Unfortunately, they were not a lot of help until we taught them how to apply what they had studied in school about woven and knitted fabrics to our unique requirements.

Meanwhile, outside consulting groups were pushing '*the teamwork approach*' as the ultimate answer to every ailment. Instead I've found the 'daffy-nition' of, "*A camel is a horse designed by a committee,*" to be true. Unless you have a well-coordinated group of exceptional, self-starters, nothing useful is accomplished. The results won't mesh well with a team approach.

A knowledgeable and resourceful leader is required to provide direction, so each individual can maximise output and the results of their efforts can be properly integrated. Making the most out of available resources and people support in service groups increases overall productivity further.

Another daffy-nition that seemed to be applicable was, "*An elephant is a mouse that meets US Government standards.*" It's big, unwieldy and not cost effective, so keep it simple.

NASA is like most other government agencies. On my way out the door on a last-minute trip to Houston, my boss would say, "*Now don't confuse them with logic.*"

If a problem arose, the remedy was to send a detailed report to the Manned Spacecraft Center in Houston on the situation. If you hustled, the redesign could be implemented before the next NASA review. Otherwise their micro-management would inflate the molehill and delay action on other, more critical issues. Besides, we already had enough mountains to climb on a daily basis.

One-time a NASA request caught me totally off guard. In two weeks', time, they wanted to know the full impact of the planned Skylab environment on all the Apollo gear we were supplying.

It soon became obvious that mould, fungus and bacteria growth would need to be retarded with the longer missions in space. At the time, I couldn't take my biochemist away from his projects.

Not knowing where to begin, I just started writing one paragraph after another as I did my research. It turned out that my initial beginning became the second paragraph of my fifty-page report (or as Confucius said, *"The journey of a thousand miles begins with but a single step."*).

My old NASA 'buddy' Ralph (of helmet fame) pooh-poohed my conclusions but agreed to a 90-day test to simulate a 180-day long planned mission.

Subjects would exercise in the spacesuits on a regular basis but weren't allowed to bathe to simulate time in orbit (they were not popular at parties). In between, the components would be stored in the manner NASA proposed for the Skylab Mission.

After the test completion, Ralph was the first to open the sealed containers with the Apollo gear. It turns out he didn't know he had a severe allergy to mould and ended up in the hospital. I don't remember Ralph giving me as much grief after that.

Based on the results of the test, the microbiologists came out of the woodwork. As a group, they must have been previously ignored at NASA Houston. Because organisms have been known to grow on optical lenses in the vacuum of space and on the edge of volcano vents at the bottom of the ocean, their composite reaction was there was no way to guarantee any solution would work.

Nevertheless, suit-drying stations were added to Skylab, but additional steps were still needed later on for additional fungal growth suppression.

Sonny, the Apollo Program Manager told me, *"I once hired a pattern-maker who I thought had twenty years' worth of experience. Turns out he had one year of experience twenty times. You have the opposite problem because you've never done the same thing twice."* That's what made everything challenging and a lot of fun. It meant a lot to be singled out for praise from the talented guy at the top of the in-house Apollo pyramid.

On another occasion, he commented, *"Parker, I don't know how we ended up with you, but I'm sure glad we did."* This is the same engineer who I needed to spend half a day explaining the specifics about chemicals or materials using all kinds of analogies. He had degrees in electrical and mechanical engineering. He insisted upon having all the details spoon-fed to make sure he understood all the information at hand.

Then he'd get on the phone to NASA in Houston and concisely summarise everything to them in 20 or 30 minutes without omitting many pertinent points. I was never that good with company politics or briefly explaining technical stuff to someone outside my fields.

Once he stopped me cold in the middle of an engineering meeting and said with a big grin to one of my junior engineers, "You *know that if you learn to say polyethylene, polypropylene five times fast, you can have **his** job!"* as he pointed at me.

Sonny would throw assignments at me, one after another. I'd keep him posted and file the usual progress reports to keep him abreast on what was happening. Meanwhile he'd be doing his thing. There were often times when I needed his authorisation for additional funds or having critical work done on overtime in another department to keep up with the programme schedule.

The only solution was that I'd have to find him before people started to leave for the day. I'd chase him down to get his signature as soon as he got out of a meeting once I found out where the meeting was taking place. I also needed to determine if I could interrupt to get his authorisation.

For a while I had trouble in under-communicating. When I first started with the company, I'd heard the stories of the chemist and the electronics guy who were responsible for the initial suit development and winning the Apollo Block II contract for the company. Somehow, I had the two individuals mixed up.

I kept walking into this vice president's office, assuming he was a PhD chemist who knew at least as much chemistry as I did. Skipping all the details, I would succinctly answer the questions he had called me in for. He would look at me as if I didn't know what I was talking about. I couldn't understand why he was confused until I found out he was the electronics guy and I had been doing a snow job on him for months without knowing it. My bad.

NASA had a civil servant with advanced degrees in mechanical and industrial engineering. After he completed an initial assignment, they had no idea what he could do next. They sent him up to Delaware from Houston as the NASA in-house resident engineer to approve all design and process changes on-site.

'Charlie' would come up to me and ask what a specific engineering revision was all about that I had already reviewed and approved. It seemed other people didn't want to take the time to go over all the details with him. After I explained the changes and ramifications in detail, his eyes would usually glaze over.

Because I was usually in the middle of something else, I'd switch gears and make something up that sounded simpler, but related. As he was signing off on the specifications with a satisfied grin, every engineer within earshot would be trying to hold back snickers.

At his retirement party a few years later, Charlie came weaving through a throng of people to pat me on the back and shake my hand as he said, *"You know, of all the people here, you were the only one to take the time to explain things in detail. It made my job a lot easier and I wanted to be sure to thank you for it."*

It should come as no surprise that we had hired many retired military people to work on government programmes. They understood what was required for delivery on military contracts.

The Apollo Contracts Administrator (Stan) was a fighter pilot in the black squadron during the Korean War. He was shot down three times. The last time he had so many bullet holes in him, they sent him home to die. Somehow, he managed to pull through.

Stan fancied himself a word merchant, perhaps because of his mother's influence as a Professor of English Literature. He would always nit-pick the wording in my reports and proposals.

He would especially get upset when I would coin a new word or phrase. Once he insisted I change my *'solvated by'* expression to read *'dissolved in solvent with'*. About six months later, I showed him a copy of a DuPont new product report that said,

"Solvated by." He just frowned and flicked his fingers, as if that would push the DuPont words off the page.

I mentioned to him that I splurged for my first colour TV when they dropped the price to $217. I had agreed to buy one when the price dropped to $200, but this was close enough. Later on, in the conversation I commented that he *"got a nice 'tan' on vacation"*. He grinned when he responded with, *"This model comes in living, breathing colour,"* as he pulled up his shirtsleeve to demonstrate.

The United States had a policy of 'buy American' for all military and government purchases so we won't get caught short in another war without access to critical materials and equipment. I felt bad about buying a 1968 TV from Japan since they refuse to purchase an equal monetary share of our products.

As co-workers, Stan and I were good friends. I was deeply saddened when he died of a heart attack at the age of forty-two.

Chapter 19
Russians-R-Coming

On July 29, 1955 President Dwight D. Eisenhower announced the United States would launch a satellite during the International Geophysical Year (1957/1958). From October 4, 1957, the US was in a space race as part of the cold war with the launch of a two-foot diameter Soviet satellite called Sputnik (Fig. 19).

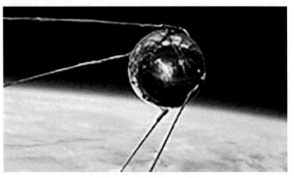

(Figure 19) Sputnik

The driving force on our part was a real concern that the Soviets could drop bombs and rockets on the United States from earth orbit or the moon and we wouldn't be able to stop it.

The Russians kept their failures a secret. They boasted of their successes after the fact, but they were the first to:

1. Put a satellite in orbit.
2. Put a man in orbit.
3. Put two men in orbit.
4. Put a female cosmonaut in space.

5. Crash land a spacecraft on the moon.
6. Soft land a spacecraft on the moon.

Meanwhile the US press televised every failure we had in real time. We had a lot of them. We progressively put Alan Shepard into space in Project Mercury followed by many others. The crew modules had limited space, so the initial astronauts selected were small. The requirements for the Mercury seven were:

"Although NASA planned an open competition for its first astronauts, President Dwight D. Eisenhower insisted that all candidates be test pilots. Because of the small space inside the Mercury spacecraft, candidates could be no taller than 5 feet 11 inches and weigh no more than 180 pounds. Other requirements included an age under 40, a bachelor's degree or the professional equivalent, 1,500 hours of flying time, and qualification to fly jet aircraft."

There were so many switches, knobs and dials that mobility to reach them all was critical. Sensors were even designed to activate by the amount of white showing in their eyeballs. Later on, this technology was adapted for paraplegics to start, stop and turn their wheelchairs.

Pressure transducers were miniaturised to monitor the astronauts' vital signs in flight. There were adapted to be inserted into veins and threaded up to the heart to determine the cause of vascular problems without major surgery.

In Project Gemini, we sent up pairs of astronauts to practice separations of the lunar module from the command/service modules and docking. Space walks (extra-vehicular activities or EVAs) determined the extent of capabilities of the astronauts to make emergency external repairs and study the effects on them with only the spacesuits as protection from environmental extremes.

The Hubble Space Telescope's mirror defects (halo fuzziness) were corrected by astronauts on 1993 EVA to produce images such as Figure 20. Hubble servicing and equipment upgrades were performed on subsequent missions to add additional capabilities.

The next logical step after project Gemini was to go to the larger Saturn V rockets to launch the Apollo Program with a three-man crew.

(Figure 20) View from Hubble Telescope

Chapter 20
Apollo 1 Fire

Due to an electrical fire in the Command Module of Apollo 1 on the Cape Canaveral launch pad during a practice run in January for a February lift off, we lost three astronauts. The hatch couldn't be opened in time to get them out.

The Command Module entrance was later reconfigured and explosive bolts were added for rapid egress, but it basically set the programme back almost two years with all the redesigns and confirmation tests.

Although the remaining astronauts grieved for the loss of Gus Grissom, Ed White and Roger Chaffee, they knew Gus, Ed and Roger would have wanted the other astronauts to continue with the programme they had all started together.

NASA had decreed everything had to be non-flammable in the pure oxygen atmosphere used for the US flights into space. Unfortunately, even steel and aluminium burn in that environment. The Russians were using a nitrogen/oxygen blend with their larger rockets and higher payloads, but that would have increased our launch and fuel weight. Then one possible result would be the astronauts experiencing the bends upon re-entry that divers contract when coming up too rapidly from deep ocean submersions.

NASA only had two materials that didn't burn in pure oxygen at that time. One was a chrome/nickel metal alloy called Chromel R ® that is used in toaster oven elements. It was drawn down to a fine filament, bundled and twisted into a yarn. When woven into a fabric, the cloth was very heavy (one pound per square yard). The other material was a Teflon® type of fluorocarbon elastomer (carboxy nitroso rubber) that had all the strength of wet chewing gum and doesn't cure (harden).

In the first meeting after the fire, out of frustration I told NASA, *"Sand doesn't burn either, but try making a flexible garment out of it."* Even though we thoroughly understood their situation, NASA was asking for the impossible to be done without adequate time or funding to make it happen. This was typical of all our space projects on the Apollo Program.

From this starting point, we began our mad dash to introduce experimental materials into production as soon as we proved they could meet the new design criteria without messing up flight schedules.

There were many long days and nights, but it was exhilarating and a lot of fun. At the end of each day, one felt a real sense of accomplishment in everyone working together to steadily advance closer to the ultimate goal of landing on the moon. One did end up with a weird sense of humour as a self-preservation mechanism to avoid getting too stressed out though.

We ultimately did find, develop and test many flame-resistant materials which were considerably safer for the astronauts.

Later we started to take a look beyond military/aerospace applications at commercial and industrial uses for fire resistant materials that we had developed and tested to meet our space needs.

An obvious one was protective suits for fire fighters. Unfortunately, it seemed that each town or city had their own druthers about the types of garments, lengths of coats, etc. They didn't want to change their minds. It didn't matter to them that standardizing would also reduce costs, so that was a blind alley.

Most aircraft crashes are survivable if the passengers can find their way out through the smoke in less than five minutes. In a study for the Federal Aviation Administration (FAA), a flameproof film hood with a drawstring provided an adequate amount of flame and smoke protection for escape within that time frame. It folded up into a small pouch to fit on the back of each airline seat or someone's pocket.

Unfortunately, the FAA decided not to specify that the airlines supply them for passengers. The FAA did place one large order so that all the FAA officials who fly could carry one. So, the next time you are in an airplane crash, the person who runs past you in the smoke with an amber-coloured plastic hood probably is on the FAA payroll.

When I contacted the interior commercial airplane designers at Boeing and McDonnell Douglas, they had their materials specified 15 years out and had no desire to change. They were not interested in switching to fire resistant sheet materials for walls, windows, ceilings and overhead bins with lower flame, toxicity and smoke generation.

They had replaced a few flammable materials in some applications with Nomex® nylon fabrics at the time but were not happy with the limited selection of colours available at that time. Since then, they have made changes to carpets, seat coverings, curtains and lower wall covering textiles.

Despite pressure from the Federal Government, flame and toxic gas protection in coal mines weren't a high priority with the mining companies either.

Chapter 21
Bodily Functions – Exhaust and Intake

A question that always seemed to arise in conversations with kids about spacesuits was, *"How do they go to the bathroom?"*

By now, it should be obvious to the reader that everything in the space programmes had an acronym. I was surprised that they had all changed between my earlier work on the Gemini Space Project and the Apollo Program. If was like taking a crash course in a new language.

UTCA is a Urine Transfer Collection Assembly consisting of a condom type sleeve, a small diameter tube and a bladder (pouch). The other component is an FCS or Fecal Containment System – basically a fuzzy, absorbent diaper.

The FCS had never been used in training or on a mission until one particularly hairy landing on the moon. There were too many rocks and craters in the way to touch down at the designated landing site before they ran out of fuel. Too much fuel used up for a controlled landing meant not being able to lift off high enough to get home to Earth.

Not mentioning any names, but a comment was made over an open microphone to NASA Mission Control in Houston that the FCS had its first field test during that descent. Fortunately, only a few of the people in the programme knew what that meant.

Another on-air discussion from Mission Control was about the unofficial Turtle Drinking Club which was formed by young American pilots stationed in England during World War II. Tradition has it that when asked the question, *"Are you a turtle?"* the correct response was, *"You bet your sweet ass I am."* Unless a satisfactory (read – very loud response so everyone could hear) answer was obtained, they would owe a round of drinks to all the other Turtle Club Members present.

Aboard a Project Mercury flight, Astronaut Wally Schirra was asked by a ground controller on open microphone, *"Are you a turtle?"* Wally switched from the radio to a flight recorder and said the long version of: "YBYSAIA" Later, on the recovery ship USS Kearsarge, they asked what his answer to the question was. Wally played it back from the flight recorder for them.

On live radio during the Apollo 7 flight, Astronaut Deke Slayton asked from Mission Control at the Houston Space Center, *"Hey Wally, are you a turtle?"* when Schirra was again in orbit. He again said the proper response on the flight recorder. Schirra was the only astronaut to fly on each of the Mercury (solo), Gemini (twins) and Apollo (three astronauts) missions.

We had a design engineer nicknamed Dixie who was working to resolve the bathroom functions in space at zero gravity. His approach was to pull a partial vacuum on a 'chamber pot'.

One day he couldn't find a place with enough privacy, so he set up behind the curtains on the stage in a large conference room. Just as he dropped his pants and the vacuum pump was going *chuga, chuga, chuga*, a company vice president walked into the room escorting a contingent of Air Force brass on a plant tour. The motorised curtains on the stage opened when he hit the light switches. Dixie didn't know what to say as they backed out of the room. We never did ask Dixie if he took a bow.

Everyone worked hard over long hours to keep up with the programme schedule, so they needed occasional diversions now and then. Dixie somehow learned he was listed in personnel files as part Native American to boost our minority count for certain government programmes. I don't think that means he's related to Senator Elizabeth Warren though. Because of that inclusion in the records, he had taken an interest in Native American culture and would give lectures at local schools clad in fringed buckskin with the full feathered headdress of a chief or sachem that he made by himself.

It so happened that many of the potato farmers on Long Island, New York had done well in selling their properties at inflated prices as building lots and moved to Maryland and Delaware to farm. During the spring ploughing season Dixie would go out and look for arrowheads. On one of these trips, another engineer named Ron asked if he could tag along. Once they set out, Dixie demonstrated his keen eye for finding one arrowhead after another on the freshly turned soil.

Ron wasn't having much luck finding arrowheads or spear points but would pick up a rock with an interesting shape or a piece of quartz every now and then. He'd ask, *"Dixie, is this any good?"*

Almost every rock he'd pick up, Dixie would say, *"That's a pup stone, it's good too,"* and Ron would throw it in his knapsack.

After a while Ron's backpack was getting heavy, when he finally asked, *"What is a pup stone and what is it good for?"*

With a big grin, Dixie said, *"They're good for chasing off any pups that stray into your yard."*

I was puzzled when I received a request for non-flammable food from NASA. I explained that for the body to 'burn' calories for conversion to energy, that by definition, food must be flammable. NASA settled for non-flammable food packaging films instead.

Chapter 22
Zipper, Foams and Helmet Trial

One of the areas in the Command Module was designated for in-flight suit storage. A flammable foam had to be replaced that held components (such as a helmet and gloves) stationary when not in use.

I considered using the flame-resistant silicone rubber used for the lunar boots, but it would add too much weight. Then I discovered a blowing agent that would convert the silicone elastomer to a flexible foam at the same temperature as the fluid silicone mixture could be processed from a liquid to a solid. The porosity greatly reduced the weight compared to the solid component.

Unfortunately, the additive manufacturer had a manufacturing plant explosion where a worker was injured, and they planned to stop making it. We placed a large enough order to make certain we had enough in stock for years to come and stored it in a walk-in refrigerator to extend the storage life.

A NASA New Technology Report is the equivalent of a US patent that makes the information available to other government contractors and the public.

Years after writing up the silicone rubber foam moulding technique, I happen to be at a manufacturer in the Mid-west who was using my process to cushion ceramic insulators to steel supports on high voltage power lines. They had purchased an adequate quantity of blowing agent to last them at least 30 years.

On my plant tour, I didn't mention to them that I was the one who developed that method. It was great to know that it was being used in commercial applications, but deep down, I felt I should have been getting a percentage of the profits resulting from my invention. Unfortunately, the government owned the rights of products and processes that I developed under the production contract. Their policy was to share the non-classified new technology with the public for private and commercial use.

One of my junior engineers had an Associate of Science degree and was going to night school to complete his bachelor's degree. I began to notice in his telephone calls to suppliers that he was able to obtain what their company's lawyers might deem to be proprietary information.

I started having him call vendors with a list of questions to ask in between anything that was almost relevant which popped into his head. If he wrote down everything he could remember as soon as he hung up the phone, I would usually have sufficient data available to be able to use their products. If I asked too many of the 'right' questions myself, they would clam up. Perhaps they assumed I wanted to go into competition with them. It was better to let them try to impress me with their knowledge.

We were having occasional trouble with the pressure-sealing zipper on the suit not sealing. I went to BF Goodrich's bicycle and motorcycle tire plant in New Bedford, Massachusetts in a hanger where blimps were once made for the military.

They were coating the rubber on fabric to be used in the suit pressure-sealing zipper on equipment that normally manufactured textile reinforced rubber printing blankets. For a change, I managed to keep my mouth shut and not ask any questions as they gave me a plant tour and explained everything in detail on the first day of the production run. I did inform them of how critical their product was to the astronauts' survival. They could not have been nicer or more accommodating.

One the second day, I started to ask things like, *"Why is the temperature on that end of the process oven much higher than yesterday?"* and *"How come the pressure gage seems to have more variability today?"* From that point on, it seemed that they could not get me out of the plant fast enough.

I did much better gleaning information when it appeared that I didn't know anything about their operation. From then on, I tried harder to not miss opportunities to keep my mouth shut. It never worked for me, but I kept trying.

Flying out to the zipper manufacturing plant in western Pennsylvania, I was greeted by a German mechanical engineer who was rightfully proud of the machine he had designed and built to attach the locking teeth to the fabric reinforced rubber sheet from the Goodrich plant in Massachusetts.

Before turning the zipper machine on and slowly starting it up, he explained how the copper alloy strips were shaped as the mating parts were simultaneously cut and attached. Of course, once it was up to speed, everything was moving so fast that it became a blur to the eye and sounded like a machine gun.

There didn't appear to be anything I could suggest to improve the operation, but at least I understood what was involved in the process.

Speaking of Murphy's Law, before I could get home from that trip, I had to spend the night at the airport in Erie, Pennsylvania because of a blizzard which wasn't in the weather forecast. Since the intermittent problems went away after my return, I assume they tightened up their internal specifications and controls.

NASA opted to use the English measuring system instead of metric (like the rest of the world). To do experimental forming of the helmets, we had a special extrusion run of low gel, optical grade resin.

The sheets were then melt polished between bright chrome plates in a heated press to improve transparency and the surface quality. Before the moulding trials could be run, the resin had to be dried overnight at **275°F** (Fahrenheit) to avoid forming bubbles from residual water in the blowing process. Unfortunately, the model shop used a centigrade (metric) thermometer. In the morning, we ended up with a big puddle of very expensive resin at the bottom of the **275°C** (Centigrade) oven (which is the same temperature as 527°F).

Even when cool, the clear polymer could not be removed from the brand new, expensive oven. There was no way to salvage the oven or the plastic, so it was a very costly trial without any benefits to show for all the effort expended.

The astronauts had been subjected to a g-force of over 7 (seven times the amount of gravity) upon re-entry on Apollo 16. Their heads and necks are supported by a stiff foam cushion (Figure 21) shaped like a cross-section of a light bulb to distribute the g-force load on their heads). Behind the foam pad is a formed aluminium support with a wide recessed groove shaped like a question mark. This spreads the flow of oxygen uniformly across the front of the helmet to minimise fogging inside the helmet and to keep the astronaut cool.

(Figure 21) Helmet Head Cushion

NASA was concerned that the variability of the porosity, apparent density and resiliency in the foam might be too broad. I tightened up the tolerances on the specification amounts of the foam components used to fill the mould and the process times. Verifying the weight of the pad and adding a foam compression test resolved the consistency question to better protect the crew in extreme flight situations.

The astronauts also needed to blow through their nose to relieve the inner ear pressure differential upon launch and re-entry. Since they can't reach their nose inside their helmet, we had to add a Valsalva device. This was a small, soft rubber cube with a 'V' slot mounted inside the helmet. Placing their nose in the slot to seal their nostrils and gently blowing relieved the pressure on the eardrum with no hands required.

Chapter 23
Fire, Beta, Rubbers, Spacers and Velcro

Many of the high-performance materials DuPont developed were incorporated or modified for use in the Apollo program to build the spacesuits and accessories. I was given the honour of participating in the joint press briefing with DuPont Corporate people at the Cape Kennedy lift-off for the Apollo 11 first moon-landing mission. I was proud to be selected for the assignment. I explained where and why the high technology materials were used.

Being given a grand tour of the Hotel DuPont in Wilmington, Delaware before my meetings with the top DuPont Corporation marketing staff in preparation for the pre-lunar launch press briefing was an amazing experience. They even had a large ballroom for debutant coming out parties with a huge chandelier and a grand staircase for debutants to make an ostentatious entrance.

I also received the Apollo Achievement Award from NASA for my contributions in getting men to the moon and back.

Pictures of me were in World Book Encyclopaedia for ten years under both *'Aerospace'* and *'Engineering'*. My sister Sue is 12 years my junior. When she showed her classmates those volumes of the encyclopaedia and said, *"That's my brother."*

They would reply, *"Yeah, right."*

There was a mechanical engineer named Rob where I worked on the Apollo Space Program. Rob said he was cheated one year when he didn't get a raise. He felt he had worked his tail off. His boss told him that he wasn't making use of the resources available to him, so he wanted to teach Rob a lesson he would remember.

Rob would work out a design and run to the model shop. Because there was a waiting list to get things done, he'd make the prototype himself. The same thing happened when he went to drafting. He'd get on a table and make the drawings, then write the process specification. Instead of putting the documents in the inter-office mail loop for signatures, Rob would hand-carry the drawings and procedures around to all the departments for approval, even if he had to wait until each meeting was finished. Otherwise he'd return later so he could get them signed that same day.

Basically, his boss had created a monster. Rob would approach everyone to pawn off his work assignments. He'd come to me and explain what he needed to be done. Then he had the nerve to ask me to do it.

I'd tell him, *"Rob, my plate is full and there was no way I have time to do your job too."*

He'd say, *"Please do it,"* over his shoulder as he walked away. After a while Rob finally learned that I wouldn't stop everything for what he was responsible to accomplish. He'd still try to delegate most of his assignments to others anyway.

When the spacesuit was inflated, it was fairly rigid. Flexing joints was akin to bending a football pressurised for someone other than Tom Brady of the New England Patriots. The solution was to make convoluted joints similar to the bellows on an accordion or a clothes dryer vent hose.

Collapsible mould cylinders were dipped in a rubber bath and covered with reinforcing fabric. Wire cables embedded in rubber were added on both sides of the cylinder to prevent longitudinal expansion. Then a rubber top layer was applied. Because of inconsistencies in the process from one operator to the next, Rob was assigned to the dip room to standardise the procedures.

In the end, Rob had written small phone book-sized detailed instructions for each process. The revised procedures for each operation were so complicated that nobody in that Production Department read or used them. Everything took a dramatic turn for the worse and output ground to a halt because of all the additional problems created.

John, the Apollo Engineering Manager called me in and asked me to fix it. I said I had too many things going on for my group that were top priority. I also told him the process was primarily water based and I didn't want to become a specialist in obsolete technology. I wasn't aware that most things would revert away from solvent-based products a few decades later to meet the new Environmental Protection Agency (EPA) requirements.

My new boss John said, "*You're the best we have and getting everything under control depends on you fixing it in a hurry.*"

Although I was flattered, I couldn't imagine how I could possibly manage what amounted to a full-time assignment and continue everything else that was on my plate.

As previously mentioned, I felt I was at least average at everything I tried to do. Since John claimed I had the best batting record at doing things right the first time and on schedule compared to the other engineers, I started to think about that. Although I decided he may be on to something there, I bombarded him with a bunch of BUTS:

"BUT, how can I keep all the projects in my group going while I am doing that?

BUT, that part of the plant is a quarter mile away across the building.

BUT, how will I be able to make all the engineering meetings on time?

BUT, BUT, BUT..."

It took six months, BUT somehow, I managed to simplify and rewrite all the procedures to reduce each of them from Rob's 20 to 30 pages to two or three essential ones for each process. Then they could be used.

I developed a stronger contact adhesive to bond the rubber, fabric and cable assembly together with a modified process. All the while I was running the length of the plant and skipping lunch to try to find enough hours in the day to keep everything else and my group going.

Meanwhile, the last shreds of everyone's patience with Rob's antics were wearing thin. We started pulling little tricks on him to get even. Taping down the little button on the cradle of his rotary dial telephone would keep the phone ringing after he picked up the transceiver. A few days later, he'd realise it had happened again after he said, "*Hello,*" for the third time.

By turning his desk around and putting his books and his in-out basket on the opposite side, he would bang his knees when he pulled his chair in to sit down. Of course, it was funnier to us when he'd keep falling for the same pranks, time and time again. Eventually, he got the point and would complete his own assignments without annoying everyone else in the process.

Because of the workloads and tight schedules, we all needed to blow off steam now and then. There was a tall, thin consulting engineer from Ling Temco Vought (LTV) Aerospace Corporation who wore dark horn-rimmed glasses and had a crew cut. He was fairly bright and on the quiet side, but without a whole lot of personality. Today he'd be classified as a nerd.

He did have a weird sense of humour though. When 'Crazy Glue' was a new thing, he'd walk up to a secretary (that's what they were called back then) and ask her to hold out a finger. He would apply a drop of adhesive on her finger, then hold her thumb down against the finger for a minute and then walk away. After sitting there for a moment wondering what just happened, she'd try to get her fingers apart and panic. Of course, the fingers had to be gently peeled apart because direct pulling would tear the skin off. He thought it was funny.

With rapid task expansion, new offices and rooms were erected in the factory area. He'd stand up on a desk on the opposite side of a partition and dangle a rubber spider on a string in front of another secretary while she was typing to get a rise out of her. His redeeming grace was that he was very good at solving design problems and helped me out on a couple of critical issues.

Following the fire on the Apollo 1 launch pad that claimed the lives of three astronauts, Owens Corning developed a super fine, flexible glass filament called Beta Fiberglas®. This was to aid NASA's effort to significantly reduce the disastrous effects of another fire involving exposure of the suit materials. It did not burn when exposed to a direct flame but melted out of the way. Unfortunately, it wasn't very durable.

The next iteration would involve sizing the glass yarn with starch to facilitate weaving. Heat cleaning the woven fiberglass would remove (burn off) the temporary starch binder before coating the fabric with PTFE Teflon®. The initial results appeared to be tough, abrasion resistant and durable on an M.I.T. flex-fold endurance-testing machine.

Upon hard crease folding even once, however, the breaking strength was found to be less than five percent of the original. Examination of the flex-tested samples revealed that the Teflon® coating would break up and work its way into the yarn fibres on the tester. This prevented abrasion between fibres, unlike what would happen in actual use.

Ultimately, we found that pre-coating the individual yarns with Teflon® before weaving would make a much tougher cloth. It had an added bonus of a significant improvement in tear strength. This configuration was dubbed 'Super Beta®' cloth and became the outermost layer in the spacesuit. Everything looked great initially. Unfortunately, over time the hardware attachments (Fig. 22 – oxygen, electrical and fluid hose connectors from the backpack) on the chest panel of the spacesuit would easily tear up the Super Beta during normal mission and training activity.

(Figure 22) Suit Interconnects

I developed a white, fluorocarbon elastomer coating with a low coefficient of friction that was flame resistant in pure oxygen (Figure 22 Interconnect Panel), but it took some doing. Changing the emissivity from the typical black carbon or tan clay filled. Teflon® like rubbers required a new approach to compounding

Increasing the reflectivity, light diffusion and opacity reduced the thermal stabilisation temperature in direct sunlight and the cooling demand of the backpack. Flexibility at cryogenic temperatures (super cold of space and the moon) was also required and it passed the cold flex 180-degree angle bend test at NASA. Incorporation of a microfine Teflon® powder in the rubber increased the abrasion resistance by smearing a very thin coating over the wear surface which reduced the co-efficient of friction.

It so happened that a need for outer wrist ring seals arose at the same time to reduce the amount of lunar dust penetrating into the ball bearings in the glove and suit arm interface. Like the helmet to neck hardware interface, the wrist joints each consist of two metal mating assemblies. They click and lock together the arm and glove hardware rings. Moulding the new white rubber over a reinforcing fabric also worked well for that application. Although the surface was slippery, I was pleasantly surprised that it was still receptive to adhesives for bonding.

The Space Shuttle Challenger disaster in 1986 reportedly was caused by an 'O' ring seal not designed for a cold launch temperature. It's possible that this new type of formulating approach for low temperature flexibility could prevent a leak from happening on future rocket launches in cold weather.

A heat cleaned Beta Fiberglas® mesh fabric (like window screen) was used between the outer layers of vacuum metalized Kapton® polyimide film for fire resistant thermal insulation. In test cycling, the ultra-fine glass fibres disintegrated to a pile of glass dust in the seams of the outer ITMG garment.

A sizing solution of a flameproof CTFE resin (chlorofluorocarbon plastic) was tested on the Beta Fiberglas® spacer fabric to prevent abrasion between the individual glass fibres. It worked great, but I couldn't find a supplier who could process it in time for the next scheduled mission.

Cutting foot long pieces of two inch by twelve-inch wooden planks to a 'U' shape, I made a wide trough from a thick Nylon®

sheet. The ends were sealed to the wood with an epoxy adhesive. Lengths of galvanized steel electrical conduit were held in place with C- clamps for use as unwind and rewind stands. Another steel pipe in the bath kept the fabric submerged in the resin solution as the rolls were unwound, dragged through the solution and then under a bank of infrared heat lamps for drying.

This was done in a new lab under construction with the windows opened and a fan used to blow in fresh air for ventilation. The plant safety people were a little bent about the Rube Goldberg (jerry rigged) set up. I assured them that it would be okay, and I had no other place where it could be run to keep everything clean. I suspect they were anxious to get out of there in a hurry (in case of potential problems) and let me finish the coating run. This was another case of doing the work first and writing the procedure after to make the flight 'hardware'.

At another company years later, I used this fabric impregnation sizing approach to scale up industrial applications with other resin systems for conveyer belts used in food processing, cotton cleaning and can sterilisation to significantly enhance conveyor belt durability from days to months.

It also made a big difference in the manufacture of fiberglass and Kevlar® laminates for chemical resistant tank linings to retrofit failed glass lined process vessels. That was after an old Greek chemist who developed the laminating process said, "*So what it peel like banana. It work fine.*" I fixed it anyway.

Raybestos-Manhattan developed a fire resistant, fluorinated rubber boot sole for the Pressure Garment Assembly (PGA suit). Because of the heavy clay loading in the formulation, the soles had a tendency to crack in astronaut training exercises. I had to use a flexible epoxy mix to bond the split soles together to extend the life of the inner boots used in training.

Velcro® (Figure 23) hook and loop closures were new for many applications where the insulated and pressurised gloves made use of snaps and buttons difficult or impossible. There were several applications for storage and mounting of gear and equipment in the command module at zero gravity. Sleeping bags with Velcro® closures and attachments would prevent the astronauts from drifting off and bumping into *'things in the night'* (like critical switches and dials) during sleep cycles.

Bonding Velcro® circles to the soles of the PGA boots allowed the astronauts to stay in place or move around on 'looped fibre carpet strips' without floating away from what they were trying to accomplish. Fire resistant versions of Velcro were also developed to meet NASA requirements.

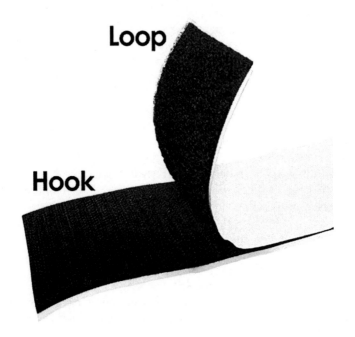

(Figure 23) Velcro

Chapter 24
First Step, Cronkite and Tactility

When I found the following article, I thought it was funny. Later I discovered that it wasn't true, but I decided to leave it in anyway.

"ON JULY 20, 1969, AS COMMANDER OF THE APOLLO 11 LUNAR MODULE, NEIL ARMSTRONG WAS THE FIRST PERSON TO SET FOOT ON THE MOON.

HIS FIRST WORDS AFTER STEPPING ON THE MOON, "THAT'S ONE SMALL STEP FOR A MAN, ONE GIANT LEAP FOR MANKIND," WERE TELEVISED TO EARTH AND HEARD BY MILLIONS. BUT, JUST BEFORE HE RE-ENTERED THE LANDER, HE MADE THE ENIGMATIC REMARK "GOOD LUCK, MR GORSKY."

MANY PEOPLE AT NASA THOUGHT IT WAS A CASUAL REMARK CONCERNING SOME RIVAL SOVIET COSMONAUT.

HOWEVER, UPON CHECKING, THERE WAS NO GORSKY IN EITHER THE RUSSIAN OR AMERICAN SPACE PROGRAMS.

OVER THE YEARS, MANY PEOPLE QUESTIONED ARMSTRONG AS TO WHAT THE 'GOOD LUCK, MR GORSKY' STATEMENT MEANT, BUT ARMSTRONG ALWAYS JUST SMILED.

ON JULY 5, 1995, IN TAMPA BAY, FLORIDA, WHILE ANSWERING QUESTIONS FOLLOWING A SPEECH,

A REPORTER BROUGHT UP THE 26-YEAR-OLD QUESTION ABOUT MR GORSKY TO ARMSTRONG.

THIS TIME HE FINALLY RESPONDED BECAUSE HIS MR GORSKY HAD JUST DIED, SO NEIL ARMSTRONG FELT HE COULD NOW ANSWER THE QUESTION. HERE IS THE ANSWER TO "WHO WAS MR GORSKY":

IN 1938, WHEN HE WAS A KID IN A SMALL MID-WESTERN TOWN, HE WAS PLAYING BASEBALL WITH A FRIEND IN THE BACKYARD. HIS FRIEND HIT THE BALL, WHICH LANDED IN HIS NEIGHBOR'S YARD BY THEIR BEDROOM WINDOW.

HIS NEIGHBORS WERE MR AND MRS GORSKY. AS HE LEANED DOWN TO PICK UP THE BALL, YOUNG ARMSTRONG HEARD MRS GORSKY SHOUTING AT MR GORSKY, "SEX! YOU WANT SEX?! YOU'LL GET SEX WHEN THE KID NEXT DOOR WALKS ON THE MOON!" IT BROKE THE PLACE UP. NEIL ARMSTRONG'S FAMILY CONFIRMED THAT THIS IS A TRUE STORY."

Walter Cronkite (1916–2009, CBS News Anchor) was referred to as *"the most trusted man in America"*. He reported extensively on the aerospace programme. When a huge poster with the picture of the footprint on the moon appeared in Grand Central Station, he said, *"Since there is no lunar wind, 500 years from now, wouldn't it be nice to know that those footprints were made by someone from the United States?"*

(Figure 24) Footprint on the moon

Of course, I got a call from NASA wanting to know how soon I could have a prototype with 'USA' on the lunar boot sole. Thinking about what was involved, I called them right back and asked if they should read *USA* or print *USA*, in which case it would read *ASU*.

After rushing a modified lunar boot sole down to Houston, they decided that it would defeat the purpose of the deep groves in the tread (Figure 24 – Footprint on the moon) that offered secure footing on the rungs of the Lunar Lander. Even though the force of gravity on the moon is only one sixth of what it is on Earth, the backpack shifts the astronaut's centre of gravity, so the grooves do make the climb much safer.

(Figure 25) Apollo 11 Crew – Armstrong, Collins and Aldrin

The Apollo 11 crew of Neal Armstrong, Michael Collins and Buzz Aldrin (fig. 25) made the trip from earth orbit to the moon in four days. Armstrong and Aldrin touched down on the lunar module (Eagle) on July 20, 1969. Armstrong was the first to set foot on the moon when he said, "That's one small step for a man, one giant leap for mankind." Collins remained aboard the command module Columbia during the first manned visit on the lunar surface.

Walter Cronkite had too much time on his hands. At a later date he mused, "*You can't tell the players without a score card when they're in space or on the surface of the moon. It would be nice to know which one the crew commander is.*"

It so happened that we previously had an abrasion problem in training exercises with the American flags mounted on the astronauts' upper arms earlier. Owens Corning had developed fire resistant acrylic inks on their Beta® fiberglass textiles for this application, but they would rub off over time.

The first thing I tried was to melt fuse a layer of clear thermoplastic FEP Teflon® film over the flag to protect it. It worked fine except for the fact that the red pigment in the flag stripes had turned brown from the heat of melt bonding. Instead I had to coat a clear silicone adhesive on the FEP Teflon® film to laminate over the flag. Problem solved.

Next, I found a high temperature resistant red pigment to be mixed into a clear silicone adhesive and laminated it to the beta fiberglass fabric to make red arm and leg bands for the commander's suit (figure 26 in Space Walk).

(Figure 26) Red Arm Bands in EVA

The same red pigment was incorporated into an epoxy resin to coat a red stripe on the commander's helmet as well. I was informed that this made Walter one happy camper.

As previously mentioned, the flameproof metal fabric was heavy, but exceptionally abrasion resistant to avoid punctures and cuts to the gloves. Unfortunately, the astronauts said the outer thermal gloves for the ITMG (insulated outer garment) with the wire cloth prevented them from turning knobs and

switches in the modules so they were only using the PGA
pressure rubber gloves inside the command and lunar modules.

An LTV consulting chemist (Joe) and I worked around the
clock to apply a flame-resistant coating by hand for all the
pressure gloves (PGA) scheduled for the next flight to be used
inside the modules.

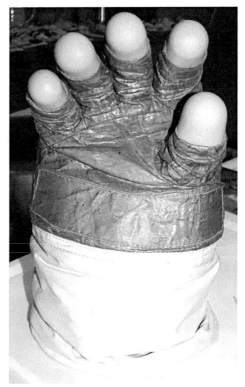

(Figure 27) ITMG glove

After that flight, I formed 10 layers of a nylon knit fabric at
a time in a heated mould to shape the reinforcing fabric into
domes (like little cowboy hats). An uncured blue silicone rubber
was applied to the individual cloth performs and moulded into
the shape of a thimble. This provided functional tactility to the
end of each finger for the lunar gloves (Fig. 27 – ITMG glove
tips).

It is gratifying when I see the same fingertips on gloves and other items I developed, designed, and tested over 50 years ago still in use today. It makes me feel as though I did a lot of things right at that time. There may have been other problems along the way, but there were enough other people who did their share to make it all work together.

Chapter 25
Apollo 13

Apollo 13 was a prime example of making do with whatever was available to rescue the astronauts from being marooned in space. Apollo 13 was scheduled to be the third landing on the moon, but the mission was aborted when an oxygen tank exploded.

Makeshift repairs to the carbon dioxide removal system made with odds and ends duct taped together helped make a return possible from space after orbiting the moon.

To save power and oxygen, the Command Module was shut down after it was decided to use the Lunar Module (LEM) as a lifeboat. Fortunately, the astronauts were able to conserve their supplies and restart the frozen Command Module again as they approached Earth.

As depicted in the Apollo 13 movie and a PBS presentation, none of this was planned or would have been possible without American ingenuity and a can-do attitude. It was a good example of in-flight improvisation that ultimately saved the crew.

Chapter 26
Bladder, Beaver Tail and Buffing

Following design changes, requalification of flex routines with the torso of the pressure garment assembly (PGA) ran into a major problem. The suit bladder consists of a rubber coating on a high tenacity nylon® fabric that behaves like an inner tube on a bicycle. During the manned cycle tests, the Neoprene® rubber was delaminating from the fabric and tearing. The test lab and I could only duplicate the effect on a test jig at a much higher rate of speed than would be encountered for any of the mission requirements.

That's when I found out the suit test subjects were performing a '*relay race*' to try to finish the tests as soon as possible to meet other schedules. These guys were young and athletic. One would don a spacesuit and go through the cycles as fast as he could. As soon as he was tired out, the next guy would jump in the same suit and take his turn. So much frictional heat was generated at the rapid cycle rates; they were melting the tie coat (primer) that anchored the rubber to the nylon® fibres. Maintaining this pace would be impossible for an astronaut to do in space at zero gravity. Slowing down the test to a more realistic rate eliminated the 'failures.'

Right after that, we encountered a shipping problem with the lower suit cables that provided the astronauts with leverage and '*frictional brakes*' to maintain the desired leg extremity positions. These restraint cables ran through what was known as a '*beaver tail*', (because of its shape and location). It resembled a translucent version of a sheath that a roofer could use to hang a hammer or hatchet on his tool belt.

During a shipment of a completed spacesuit assembly in an '*ocean liner steamer trunk*' type of container, the polypropylene beaver tail fractured. The only way I could duplicate this failure was bending it over onto itself at low temperature. That was the way it was folded in the case for shipment to NASA in Houston. One clue of what caused the problem was that it happened in the middle of a winter cold spell. Polypropylene is noted for it's unique 'hinge effect benefits' but doesn't fare well at low temperatures. This was confirmed by testing at the low winter temperatures on the loading dock in Delaware where the original material would crystallise and snap during bends

Switching to an 'alloy' of two plastics (a polyethylene modified polypropylene copolymer) inhibited crystallisation. This increased the impact fracture resistance at cold temperatures by a factor of over 20 times. The one snag was that I couldn't find any sheet stock available and there wasn't time to have it made for the next scheduled flight. Sheets of material were formed when I heated up pellets of the new resin alloy in a preheated press between metal plates with shims to control the thickness. I made enough sheet stock for thermal forming of parts in time for the upcoming mission. After that we ordered sufficient quantities of extruded replacement sheet material well in advance of our future needs.

In the pre-flight design review of engineering changes, my 'old buddy Ralph' came up from NASA Houston with his boss and a couple of his fellow project engineers. I think we decided that 'N.A.S.A.' meant 'Never A Straight Answer' because of Ralph.

After far too many of Ralph's interruptions to the proceedings, I explained how the material had failed and that was corrected by the change in raw material for the part.

Following many needless interruptions to the proceedings earlier by Ralph, he demanded to know, *"How can you tell how it failed?"*

Before I could explain that the cold fracture test edges were identical to the failed material, our Apollo Program Manager was on his feet and turning red in the face when he emphatically said, *"He can tell. He can tell! Now let's get on with the rest of the agenda so we can finish today."* It was comforting to know my boss had that much faith in me. Very quickly we were on to the next item of the overall design review.

In the early days of high altitude flying and the space programme, *'high impact'* acrylic was used for facemasks, helmets, visors and aircraft canopies. It was replaced by polycarbonate (PC) for greater impact strength and to be bullet proof for small calibre weapons, but at a sacrifice in abrasion resistance.

In astronaut training exercises, the PC plastic took quite a beating where the surface scratches and gouges began to limit the astronauts' vision. Because the helmets used in mission simulations were expensive to produce, we had to develop a polishing technique to remove the scratches accumulated without a sacrifice in optical properties.

We tried jewellers' rouge and automotive rubbing compounds used to buff metals and paint, but they were far too abrasive. I had to mix up a paste with a soft silica compound to restore the surface smoothness and optics. It was one more thing I was proud of accomplishing and glad to have off my to-do list. PC is also used for auto head light covers and is subject to developing a haze from abrasions due the rain, sandstorms, hail, sleet and pebble impacts. Now commercial versions are available to buff the auto lenses, so they do not require costly replacement.

Chapter 27
Apollo 17 Slow Down Phase – 1972

The Apollo 17 flight was the last mission to land on the moon. Congress seemed to think that the threat of Russians being able to rain things that go boom down on us from orbit or a base on the moon without challenge was diminishing. The Feds started making deeper cuts to NASA's budget in spite of all the technological achievements that resulted from the space programmes.

The United States was finally recognised as the world leader in aerospace science and exploration. NASA had achieved most of the goals set out at the onset of the manned flight space programmes.

1. We can get to space and place satellites in orbit.
2. We can survive for extended periods in orbit.
3. External repairs could be made to spacecraft and satellites (such as the Hubble telescope) by astronauts during EVAs (Extra Vehicular Activities).
4. Separation of modules and redocking can be accomplished in space.
5. Landing on the moon and lift-off to re-join the command module for earth return can be accomplished.

In the early days of the space programmes, you solved one problem after another and then jumped on the next major task screaming for attention.

At this point we had to test the old configuration AND the potential replacement ten times more than we did on the original version to prove beyond a shadow of a doubt that the change was at least ten times better. Spending more time writing than doing wasn't my idea of fun or productivity. On top of that, much of our time was now consumed writing proposals and responding to Requests for Quotations (RFQs), in triplicate for the government of course.

John, the Apollo Project Engineering Manager approached me one day and said, *"You know if you want to consider starting your own business someday, I'd be more than willing to give you all my life savings for start-up money."*

Obviously, I was surprised and flattered. Coming out of the blue, it was unexpected, and I didn't know what to say. I told him, *"Your confidence in me is appreciated, but I have two kids to get through college. I don't know how I could possibly afford to do that without a steady income. It's not that I haven't thought about running my own business, but I'd have to wait until they both graduate."* He said, "L*et me know if you change your mind."*

Meanwhile, I was starting to run out of excuses to stay in Delaware. The land was so flat, you could stand on a box in your back yard and see the whole state. Growing up in the hills of New England, I wasn't cut out to be a flatlander. When I went home to visit in central Massachusetts, it felt like the car was going to tip over backwards on the small hills I once thought nothing about peddling a bicycle over.

The centre of Delaware is surrounded by marsh in the Atlantic east coast and the Chesapeake Bay on the west side. My son's paediatrician said, "The Del Mar VA (Delaware, Maryland, Virginia) peninsula area is the worst place for Paul to be with his allergies." Paul did improve when we relocated to higher altitudes in Vermont.

The water at the coastal beaches in Delaware was slimy algae green and loaded with jellyfish. One of my technicians (a Delaware native) was a diving enthusiast. Dick said he would enter fishing contests with a snorkel. He would have to push all the silver dollar-sized jellyfish out of the way before he surfaced so they didn't sting his exposed skin around the mask and wet suit. If, he did inhale one of those little suckers through his snorkel, it would really burn on the way down.

The local seafood was so dirty and bland compared to New England's. It was over-spiced at restaurants to compensate. One of the favourite gathering places for company parties was called The Crab Shack near the beach. I got sick the first time I ate soft-shelled crabs there, so I ordered pizza after that. It did make me appreciate the seafood in Massachusetts that much more though. In all fairness, there were a few excellent seafood restaurants in Delaware and Maryland. I only like the crabs that taste like lobster though.

I did have a problem with the company's policy on promotion to management. I had all kinds of responsibility without specifically designated authority. I also felt I was not receiving appropriate compensation for my contributions to the company's success. That didn't stop me from usurping as much authority as I needed to complete any task, and nobody ever gave me grief about that. Usually I was making necessary decisions for people that should have but didn't want to stick their necks out and do their job.

Harry was a guy about my age. He lived down the street from me and worked in Production Management. He had majored in economics. He appeared on either TV's '*I've got a Secret*' or '*What's my Line*' claiming that he made spacesuits for a living. I don't recall his function because he didn't say much in meetings. I was surprised that he was able to obtain financial backing to start up a plastics moulding business. As far as I knew, he didn't have any experience in the field.

I do remember a co-worker telling me he had dropped by to see Harry and was given a tour of the business. Harry was proud to display all the latest equipment, new office furniture, fresh carpeting, etc. Months later, I heard his company went bankrupt.

Then I was really flabbergasted that he found financing again for a second time and that start up went down the toilet too. My memory is foggy on this, but he may have completed a third cycle as well. You'd think he'd have come to ask me for advice since I was an expert on plastics.

I had another neighbour who was also a chemical engineer. He happened to be afraid of certain chemicals. Adam was in separate group for our company, but we shared a lab at times. For example, he was convinced that Borax Laundry Detergent caused skin cancer and Johnson & Johnson's Micrin Mouthwash could cause oral cancer. Adam had nine kids and happened to be at least 400 pounds. His doctor told him that he wouldn't live another ten years if he didn't take off a significant amount of weight soon.

At any rate, there was a solvent I needed for a new project I was working on in the lab. Every time I opened a bottle, it would be gone the next day and I'd have to order more. I couldn't imagine what was going on until I found out that Adam was burying it out by the railroad track.

Centuries ago, this particular reagent would become unstable and could explode. That was until they discovered that a piece of iron wire immersed in the liquid eliminated the reaction and the danger. Now they have much better stabilizers. Apparently, Adam was unaware that the modified chemical was now stable, or he didn't believe it.

The solution was that I had to keep the bottle locked in my file cabinet until the project was complete. Out of sight out of mind. If Adam didn't know I was still using it, he didn't need to be afraid it might explode.

In a 1969 book, Dr Laurence Peter and Raymond Hull theorized that workers get promoted to the level where they are incompetent and remain there for the rest of their careers. 'Peter Principle' aside, it just seemed that because of my relatively young age, they thought that if I was a great technical whiz, then I couldn't possibly be exceptionally good as a full-fledged manager at the same time.

In the Vietnam era, the hippies had a saying that, "*You can't trust anybody over 30.*" Maybe the 'Greatest Generation' didn't trust anyone under 30 since I was just short of that milestone. Perhaps they figured they couldn't come up with an adequate replacement if I was promoted. Another possibility was that because I was already serving in a management capacity, why would they pay me accordingly if they didn't need to?

I finally decided to accept a position as Marketing and Product Development Manager at a company in upper New York State. It was only a few miles from the Vermont line and the Green Mountains, so I could get plenty of skiing in. When I gave my notice, ILC kept asking what it would take to get me to stay to develop new commercial and consumer products to reduce their dependency on the cyclical nature of government programmes.

The cost of living and taxes in Delaware were low, but my salary was marginally average for a decent engineer, let alone a group supervisor. I was getting raises during slow business periods when others were not, but again it didn't reflect what they implied I was worth to the company.

I ended up telling them I had already accepted the position. I said that if they came up with a 30 percent raise plus the staff and the equipment I needed to accomplish what they wanted to do; I'd consider it. The negotiations went on for a couple of weeks. They weren't coming up with much in the way of acceptable counter offers, however.

Finally, the decision was left up to a Vice President who I didn't think was capable of deciding what was in the best interest of the company. He finally said, "*No,*" after a few days of deliberation. I read him the riot act about putting me through all the bargaining meetings if they weren't serious about making me an offer I couldn't refuse and walked out.

Chapter 28
After Space Encore Career Path

What does an aerospace engineer do at the end of a space programme?

After my first decade in research and development for industry, it became obvious that sales and marketing people in this country were promoted on the basis of dropping prices to meet their sales quotas, regardless of their ability or contribution to the firm. Good or exceptional technical people were marginally pacified financially.

One division of a company I worked for would lay off all their research and development staff to save money if it didn't appear their division would meet the profit margin goals for the year. Unfortunately, that happened almost every year and they went out of business trying to sell the old products without upgrades to meet new market requirements and the competition.

Years after trying to become a valuable and exceptional scientist, I learned that there are 70:30 ratio rules. In the United States, less than thirty percent of management have sufficient technical background to understand the details of how the products are being made, what the alternative options are and what the competition is doing differently. In Europe, over seventy percent of management come from scientific or technical backgrounds.

The end result was that I went to night school taking courses in accounting, marketing and business finance so I could be considered for promotion to upper management. It didn't always work. I'd accept a position as sales, marketing or product management only to run into technical problems. I had to address these issues before I could do what it said on my job description.

The same applied to new product development and product upgrades.

Once I became a general manager and turned a start-up company around financially, I was promoted to president and director. I was bumped up in salary, but the work was boring by comparison to exclusively being a technocrat. I was good at running a business, but it wasn't fun. Granted I could still do both, but the amount of paperwork, red tape and regulations involved on just the business end was non-productive and could be handled by someone else. In my next position, I reverted to Technical Director and Product Line Manager. It was fun again.

Chapter 29
Oak Industries

As the funding wound down on the Apollo Program, I accepted a corporate marketing position in new product development at Oak Industries in Hoosick Falls, New York. It was only five miles away from a house in Vermont that was nearing completion.

The five-company group was the world's largest processor of Teflon. The Teflon technology and high-performance tapes were profitable with respectable business performance, but the growth rate was slightly less than the rigid circuit board and flex circuit divisions.

The 20-year-old company group had broken into high performance materials markets by their initial hard work, but they were resting on their laurels. When I arrived, their competitors were eating their share of the market by dropping prices and selling inferior products. I fixed Oak's technical problems for their customers and helped them break into new applications.

It was not too long before I was helping to solve production problems and upgrading existing product lines as well. My start up efforts on new product development lacked technical support. I ended up making prototypes, running tests and making trial production runs before I could start up the marketing effort with the field sales group.

Standard practice in the coated fiberglass fabric industry was to use yarns coated with starch to minimize fibre breakage in processing. When Teflon top coated conveyor belts are exposed to steam for food can sterilisation, the starch would dissolve, and the water would blow the Teflon coating off as the glass fibres abraded each other. The same effect would allow grease from microware cooking of meat to penetrate the coating which was a no-no for the United States Department of Agriculture (USDA) inspectors. Disguising the problem by adding a dye to hide the problem was not acceptable either. Heat cleaning to remove the starch before coating was not the answer for durability.

An open mesh, coated belt for cotton cleaning took a couple of days to install and lace together but wouldn't last much longer than that at the customer's facility. Heat cleaning and use of a primer coating that would melt into the fibre before top coating was in service over five months at last count. Similar results were obtained for the other belt applications and for belts used for cooling extruded plastics through in water troughs.

Clamps and thick bonded layers in continuous conveyor belting loops created problems in use. I devised a seamless belt manufacturing process that did not involve a thickness increase at the butted ends which improved tracking.

I was hired by a marketing manager who was a mechanical engineer, but he was soon 'Shanghaied' to start up a printed circuit board operation in South Korea. Because of my initial successes, he decided I should manage all product development and upgrades, not just market new products.

Meanwhile the house completion in Vermont was dragging. When the water supply hose to our camping trailer froze, we had to do the motel bit. It wasn't long before the house was almost ready, and I was trying to paint outside in the dark with a floor lamp before it became too cold at night. Two coats of paint applied in low lighting conditions hopefully covered all the bare spots.

It so happened one division had obtained a licence from a fluorocarbon resin (PVDF) supplier to make fabric reinforced laminates to reline failed glass lined chemical process tanks. Of course, the welding equipment designed for unfilled plastics directed the heat to the sheet and not the welding rod. With fabric-reinforced composites, we needed to reverse that to make it work and add a reinforced cap strip.

On a trip to train a converter in Canada how to weld laminate, I was returning through customs at the airport. They asked, "*What is in the metal box?*" Tired after a hectic trip I replied, "*It's a welding GUN,*" quickly realising that wasn't the right term in this situation. After being hauled off to another room to demonstrate it was only a hot air welder, I was released barely in time to catch my flight home.

An old Greek chemist who developed the high solids, solvent dispersion process came up to the plant to discuss the details. He said, "*So what it peel like banana. It work good!*" That logic didn't seem to make sense for a laminate made to serve as a chemical barrier to protect carbon steel vessels from chemical corrosion.

Using the sizing (primer) technique to melt encapsulate the fibres I developed on the Apollo Program, I came up with a dilute solution blend of the same resin that would penetrate the glass fibres in the fabric to lock them in place and fill the voids before application of the dispersion top coat.

Because Kevlar is resistant to hydrofluoric acid and fiberglass is not, the same method was used with Kevlar® reinforcements. Unfortunately, the first Kevlar® laminate we tried to trim with an expensive blade intended for sheet metal bent.

We were one of General Electric Silicones' biggest accounts. The president of one of our divisions had a degree in chemistry with an MBA but had worked in marketing for the oil industry. Bill and I went over to G. E. Silicones Division to discuss recent problems with their products.

I was surprised to be seated at a long conference table of chemists and chemical engineers. I think they were all PhDs. I assumed they had assembled their brain trust to help us out. We were one of their largest customers. After a while it seemed I was doing all the talking for our company.

On the way back, Bill said, "*I thought you were bullshitting them, but they kept answering you.*"

The next week we were attending a management seminar in Boston together. Bill had purchased one of the first BMWs when they were transitioning from motorcycles. He couldn't get it tuned right. On the way home through the mountains in Vermont it coughed and sputtered so much I didn't think we were going to make it home.

That was after the last time we went to the moon in Apollo 17, so BMW has come a long way since then too. I'm still driving American vehicles, however.

The main company building in town was built on a landfill hill. We had huge bug zappers outside because it was on top of an old dump. To be continuous, the roofline on the higher portion of the building resulted in a half-upper floor inside. I assume that was important to the original architects.

We ended up raising that portion of the roof to install a corporate research and development laboratory and my office on the new third floor. The picture windows provided a panoramic view of the mountains. The group president said he wanted to swap offices with me because of the improved scenery offered by the higher elevation.

It should be noted that some of the silicone technology I developed on the Apollo Space Program was useful in making high performance tapes and adhesives for industry.

Chapter 30
Sheldahl

I had made good technical progress and established excellent working relationships in New York State. An attractive offer in Minnesota surfaced to get back into marketing instead of being all things to all people.

The company considered themselves 'technical opportunists'. Among many other things, they built inflatables for space exploration, diaphragms for firing missiles from submarines, insulation joints for the Alaskan pipeline and accordion type military shelters. Each of their blimps on a rope were used to broadcast telecommunications to replace up to ten ground relay stations in underdeveloped countries.

Just before I left Vermont a few days before Thanksgiving, I had my snow tires mounted on my station wagon. It was a good thing. A blizzard came up while I was on the New York Interstate 90 when they closed the NY Thruway.

All the exit ramps were filled with cars and trailer trucks, so I couldn't get off. I was weaving from one lane to another to get around the abandoned cars and trucks, ploughing a foot of snow as I went.

As I finally was able to get off at an exit it had started to rain. The streets in Buffalo, NY were covered with shear ice. After what seemed like forever, I got to the Pease Bridge to Canada and it was closed. Backing up, I managed to turn around and find a motel with a vacancy.

It was so windy INSIDE, that we froze all night. In the morning the bridge to Ontario, Canada was opened. As we approached Toronto, the sun came out and the roads were bare. Talk about the lake snow effect on the east side of the Great Lakes.

When I arrived in Minnesota, they were having a record drought in one section, a blizzard in another and flooding in the Red River Valley, all at the same time. If you look at a map of the United States in a road atlas, Minnesota is just left of the staples. Folding the top of Maine, all of New England could fit inside of Minnesota and have space left over.

Mark Twain once said, "*If you don't like the weather in New England now just wait a few minutes.*" Having grown up in Massachusetts, it was not unusual for the thermometer to drop to twenty degrees below zero Fahrenheit on the farm one day and start to melt the next.

In Minnesota, the temperature would hover between -20^0F and -40^0F for the whole winter. What little snow they got would never melt but would blow back and forth to create new drifts. The humidity was always so low that you'd warm up in a hurry after shovelling the driveway. With the humidity changes in New England, it'd take a week to warm up after the same exposure and duration. The chill would penetrate down to your bones.

In the summer, the weather would be as hot and humid as Houston and the rest of the states in the Great Plains – AND stay like that all summer long. The natives would say they only have three seasons: summer, winter and tornado season (which comes twice a year).

(Figure 28) Detroit Lions' Silverdome

One of my initial programmes was to pitch the Metro Dome football stadium concept for the Vikings to the joint chambers of commerce of Minneapolis and St Paul.

DuPont and Owen Corning Construction underwrote a 20-year useful life for the Silverdome roof (Fig. 28) in Pontiac, Michigan. It was made of Teflon and fiberglass for the Detroit Lions of the National Football League (NFL).

We were working with the same architect and Owens Corning Construction Company, but with Dow Corning with a silicone on Fiberglas® roof to keep out the cold winters of the great plains. Sadly, enthusiasm dragged by the twin cities to agree on the details after my presentation.

At the same time, the Sheldahl Company had contracted with a chemical firm to develop an optically clear top coating for silver-coated plate glass. This was to be used in the southwest desert to amplify solar energy to create enough temperature differential to make solar power use practical. It had to have at least a 20-year life exposed to the elements and desert sandstorms. Under a US Energy Research and Development Administration (ERDA) grant, it would provide solar thermal power system with a central receiver.

We were working on a joint effort with Sandia Labs and Rockwell International. The plan was to make first surface mirrors to avoid the solar energy and heat loss on transmission through the glass and reflection back at the barn-sized target elevated 600 feet above ground level to concentrate the solar power.

The 20-foot diameter dishes on pedestals would track the sun and offer a square mile of reflective surface to generate sufficient electricity to power 10 to 15 thousand homes (Fig. 29).

(Figure 29) Solar power

Solar power is the conversion of sunlight into electricity indirectly using concentrated solar power (CSP). Concentrated solar power systems use lenses or mirrors and tracking systems to focus a large area of sunlight into a small beam.

— Wikipedia

Unfortunately, the product supplied by a consulting firm as a clear, protective layer for the silver coating on the face side of the plate glass failed miserably. I rushed to develop an alternative that passed all the accelerated aging tests.

When we went to the world's largest mirror manufacturer in North Carolina for scale up trials, there were problems baking the coating with ovens designed for drying paint on the back of their second surface conventional mirrors.

I was elected to commute down to North Carolina from Minnesota during weekend mirror factory shutdowns to resolve the drying process problems with the ovens and run the mirror plant. Soon I had 12-foot-wide sheets of one quarter inch thick plate glass being silvered, top coated with my new clear coating formulation and cured in line at a reasonable process speed.

Logistics created other problems. At times supplies weren't delivered to North Carolina on time or we wouldn't have enough supplies on hand to last to the end of the run while I made adjustments.

Fortunately, the plant engineer was resourceful and knew all the people in the furniture manufacturing companies in the area. He could holler at his good old buddies to get replacement materials in the Bible Belt on Sunday morning, so we could finish our run and catch our plane back to Minneapolis that night.

Because he went with us in and out of the plant, we didn't seem to be 'Damn Yankees' even though we talked funny. He was a multifunctional engineer with great people skills who was pretty sharp at keeping everything running.

A foreman had worked for the mirror company for 40 years. At his retirement party he said, *"I never did like working here. I just want to buy ten acres of land to raise tobacco, pumpkins and a few horses."* Perhaps he didn't want to work at the local chicken farms or furniture manufacturers.

Having rescued the programme, we kept on schedule and usually returned to the twin cities on time. We missed our flight one Sunday night and it took seven hops over nine hours on all kinds of planes to get home. Going down a runway in the Ozarks, the cabin of a propeller driven antique plane was swaying independently of the wings on a rough runway. We were trying to beat the tornadoes predicted in a torrential downpour. Although scary, we just wanted to get home after another hectic weekend plant run.

The solar concentrator concept was also installed in a different configuration on tropical islands for distilling water and Bacardi rum. To avoid drawing in seawater from shallow island wells, this lessened the amount of drinking water that had to be brought in by ship from the mainland.

On the lunar module, the Kapton® film metallized with pure gold provided insulation for the lunar module because of gold's superior reflective properties and thermal stability. When I was at Sheldahl in Northfield, Minnesota, A government agent would follow company employees to the safe where the gold was kept.

After weighing, the agent would be on hand throughout the metallization process. The roll of film was weighed before and after the gold deposition process on the Kapton® film. The same government agent would observe the cleaning of the chamber and the weighing of the gold recovered after the deposition process was complete.

In Minnesota, my wife's major surgery was complicated by the long trips to the hospital in the twin cities without family nearby to help with the two kids while I still was working. It was decided to return to New England.

Chapter 31
Fabrics Research Labs – Space Shuttle

On the Space Shuttle Program, I refined the process to scale up coating of a silicone rubber layer to bond a caramelised felt cushion. It was used under the insulating ceramic foam tiles on the ablative heat shield outer skin of the shuttle. With proper orientation of the heat shield under the Shuttle (fig. 30) upon re-entry to the Earth's atmosphere, this protected the astronauts from the extraordinary frictional heat generated as it entered the atmosphere from space.

(Figure 30) Space Shuttle

The silicone rubber adhesive selected had been qualified for use on the Redstone rocket built by Chrysler starting in 1953.

The Redstone was used to launch the first satellite for the United States and our first two astronauts into orbit. Unfortunately, new and improved versions of the silicone product used were developed, so it was discontinued by the manufacturer. They were persuaded to keep making it for NASA programmes to avoid the costly requalification tests on an alternative.

I modified the production method sufficiently to compensate for the process problems. This was primarily due to the high viscosity of the original raw material specified by NASA at Fabrics Research Laboratories (FRL) of Albany International in Dedham, Massachusetts. Additional pressure on the coating head apparatus to inhibit deflection resulted in a more uniform cross section.

I also resolved problems for laundry durable, printed cloth labels for clothing.

Years later NASA was having trouble with the ceramic tiles cracking and falling off the Shuttle. I sent them a letter explaining how to solve the problem. A few years earlier I was working on cleaning procedures for ceramic recording heads (computer chips) used in computers. I found that ultrasonic cleaning would only reveal a problem with defective components, such as small flaws which later could develop into component crack failures. Using ultrasonic to detect damaged tiles would reduce the probability of the tiles coming off in flight, but I never heard back from NASA.

One of my resumes from Minnesota had found its way to a start-up company in Holyoke, MA. They competed with the 3M Company in the manufacture of high-performance tapes and film adhesives for durable goods and needed a general manager. DPI had tried to turn the profitability corner for seven years without success. After I gave my notice at the FRL Division, Albany International scrambled to find me a comparable position in their organisation. Apparently, they were extremely happy with my performance. I was pleased to have been able to contribute to the Shuttle effort, but I explained that I had already accepted an offer.

Chapter 32
Dielectric Polymers

DPI was overwhelmed with technical problems which I resolved the first year and turned the company around. Unfortunately, by solving supplier problems, I helped out 3M and other competitors sharing those same suppliers.

I was promoted to President and Director of DPI based on my efforts.

We developed a number of film adhesive and tape products to round out the product line. Next, we added tapes for chemical etch masking and soldering of electronic circuit boards. Heat sealable film adhesives were adapted for banding US currency and automotive products.

The high-rise Sears Building in Chicago started dropping architectural glass plates on the sidewalk with expansion and contraction. Spotters with binoculars and walkie-talkies (radios) were employed on the opposite side of the street to clear the sidewalks when a glass pane fell. We developed a protective mask to hold insulated single layer glass together for elevator shafts and utility areas of glass curtain walled buildings.

(Figure 31) Curtain Wall Architecture

A curtain wall system is an outer covering of a building in which the outer walls are non-structural, but merely keep the weather out and the occupants in. As the curtain wall is non-structural it can be made of a lightweight material, reducing construction costs. When glass is used as the curtain wall, a great advantage is that natural light can penetrate deeper within the building.

— Wikipedia

An electro-optical company needed an optically clear process tape to manufacture LEDs (light emitting diodes). Our custom-made product developed for them was the only one that worked out of 28 companies they contacted. Imagine my surprise when an Asian trading company ordered the item by our part number when we only had the one customer.

As a small company selling to competitors of sister companies we were also supplying, we still managed to grow sales volume based on improved product performance over the competition. Sales to other industries and markets also helped us grow in sales volume.

Taking the sales, marketing, planning, government compliance and union issues in stride left little time for my love of invention, research and development. While I was glad to have done better than my predecessors in running the company, seven years later it seemed like I was on an endless treadmill. Trying to do too much myself with not enough hours in the day, I was receptive to an offer as Technical Director for a start-up company in Connecticut with a portion of the net proceeds promised as an incentive.

Chapter 33
Web Technologies

A metallized, coating and laminating firm in Connecticut processed films for graphic arts and food packaging. In addition to being Technical Director, I was made Product Line Manager for electrostatic protective packaging for sensitive electronic components.

I did colour matching and adhesive formulations. The adhesive and coating experience in the space programmes provided a good starting point for many of my formulations at Web. I made static dissipative and electrically conductive coatings as well as adhesive formulations for electronic and medical component packaging products which were growing well in sales volume.

At a time when the overall business climate was slowing down, I worked with a laser manufacturer to develop a coating to make bar codes. Unfortunately, that was one application I failed to develop an economically viable answer in the time allotted.

Coating experience with rotogravure presses helped with the high-speed printing on the same type of equipment in my next position at Dennison.

Chapter 34
Dennison Manufacturing

I was surprised when I interviewed that they wanted to see a representative cross-section of my US patents and New Technology Reports for NASA. For me that was a first. The Corporate Executive Vice President wanted a manager of a New Chemical Technology Group in the Advanced Development Division to direct corporate new product development efforts and assist the divisions with their product upgrades as well as problem resolution.

The company had been around for over 150 years but had stagnated somewhat after significant investment in ion deposition printing. The divisions seemed to take the following mottos seriously regarding change:

"Not invented here."
"Tried it years ago, didn't work."
"We've always done it that way."

The Therimage (thermal imaging) Division reverse printed heat transfer labels on a wax-coated paper. The major toiletries and cosmetic firms were unhappy that the hot wax used in transferring the pre-printed labels would scuff in shipment and produce an irregular halo effect on their products. I formulated a plastic coating to eliminate the wax. The hot coating would still conform to the irregular curvature of blow moulded bottles and injection moulded containers but stay behind on the carrier. That way, the graphics would remain as sharp as the protective lacquer would permit. My new boss said with a chuckle that, *"The new approach was so good, the division will have to use it."*

The major cosmetics firms also didn't like the dull metallic inks on their labels. They had been requesting a product with better shelf appeal for years. My experiences with metallized films, fabrics and insulation on aerospace and military programmes were useful in these efforts as well. We developed and patented a heat stable protective coating lacquer for bright metal transfers for the same division. The new graphics caught the eye and stood out compared to the competitive products in the store. The Division General Manager remarked about our group efforts, *"Thanks for all your help. You guys are a breath of fresh air."*

The Metallized Paper Division started up ten years earlier making gift wrap and packaging materials. One project they had on a back burner a long time was diffraction embossing and holograms. We demonstrated a production process with new coating formulations and applied for patents within my first year. With the new products, it wasn't long before that division was profitable for the first time. After the merger with Avery, the Metallized Paper Division was sold to Van Leer.

We had a corporate lunch bunch in Framingham, MA consisting of six to eight guys, depending on who was available. One day we were out to eat lunch at an Italian restaurant on a Friday having a glass of wine. Since the group was primarily technical, we were talking about hollow fibres used for filtration. Most organics are composed of hydrocarbons. I raised the question, *"Why don't they make hollow fibres from hollow carbons instead?"*

Dick (another punster in the group) asked, *"What does a holocaust?"*

I said, *"You'd have to find a bean counter from the Ozarks who knows the difference between a holler (valley) and a waller (pig sty)."*

The Vice President of Corporate Marketing asked one day over lunch, *"Wouldn't it be nice to place a meal in a microwave oven and have it all cook perfectly at the same time?"*

Lightly metallized film and papers have been used for some time to accelerate the yield of popcorn plus browning and crisping of potpies and pizza in microwave ovens. Unfortunately, everything doesn't cook well at the same time and temperature in a microwave oven.

Microwave

Microwaves are a form of electromagnetic radiation with wavelengths ranging from one meter to one millimeter; with frequencies between 300 MHz (100 cm) and 300 GHz (0.1 cm). This broad definition includes both UHF and EHF (millimeter waves), and various sources use different boundaries.

– Wikipedia

We developed and patented semi conductive inks which could be printed in patterns to control the temperatures. A competitive product had run-away heating which could start fires in the ovens. We had been working with a major food company until they underwent a merger with a European firm and stopped the programme. By the time we started working with other food companies, Dennison merged with Avery. That brought many projects to a screeching halt. I once wondered if this chemistry would absorb the radiation emitted by the radar guns on the highway if it were used as a car undercoating. Are cloaking devises legal? They could also be used in stealth aircraft when skies are overcast.

Before the Framingham, MA, operations were essentially shut down or sold, I was asked to transfer to the Avery Corporate R&D Lab in Pasadena. Having wasted too much time on business trips through the years in the airports and on stalled interstate highway traffic in California, I said, *"I have no interest in moving there."*

I contacted a former customer in Seattle of one of my previous companies to secure a position for a chemist. He ended up as Research and Development Director. Avery Dennison did find positions in other locations for most of my group.

While looking for alternate employment in a commutable range, I was contacted by a Dennison corporate attorney in Waltham, MA. She insisted that I couldn't go to work for a competitor because of restrictions in the Avery employee-hiring contract. I informed her that it is illegal to prevent individuals from practicing their trades and that I didn't sign that agreement. I also informed her that most of what I did, I had learned or developed long before coming to Dennison. Almost all of my encounters with Avery Dennison technology was fixing it. The numerous patents I filed for Dennison were developed by me and

157

my group. Problems I solved for Dennison improved or replaced old technology.

The harassment by the lawyer continued. I didn't want to engage in a long, drawn out legal skirmish with them or involve a new employer. Although Digital Equipment Corporation lost $4 billion the prior year, they were located in the same town where I lived which shortened my commute time considerably. DEC assured me that the division was one of two profitable operations, so I accepted the positions of Group Leader and Senior Hardware Engineer.

Chapter 35
Digital Equipment Corporation

Digital Equipment (DEC) in Shrewsbury, MA manufactured wafers to make computer chips for read-write printing heads. I was offered a position on a Friday to start on the following Monday. Based on discussions during the interviews, I hand wrote proposals for new projects to resolve a couple of their major technical problems over the weekend.

After being introduced to many different individuals on my first day, I handed the proposals to the secretary of the group for typing. After a puzzled look appeared on her face, she said, *"What are you giving them to me for?"* Apparently, she was the only secretary for over 500 people. They still didn't call them administrative assistants back then.

I had never been in a position before where an engineering manager was expected to type, let alone try to work in a tiny cubical like Dilbert. Another problem right off the bat was that I knew nothing about Digital's Vax computer systems. Eventually I learned to type with three fingers and a thumb while watching the keyboard, but at that time I could write in longhand or dictate faster than I could type. In typing, I had to concentrate on how to use the computer instead of what I was writing. Having a skilled typist available would have been much more cost effective and productive. What is wrong with these computer people and their thought process?

Before the end of the first day, they wanted me to purchase millions of dollars' worth of production equipment immediately to replace an older, fully automated robotics process line that was never set up for use or turned on. It seems the engineer who purchased the automated machinery was always too busy to arrange for installation after the new process equipment was delivered. I asked them, *"How can I do that when you don't know what you need to fix the process,"* but they were insistent.

One of the mechanical engineers from another division had just retired and was reincarnated as a consultant over the same weekend. He was bent out of shape because I said, *"It would take six months of testing to determine exactly what type of equipment was needed."* I told him, *"You've got to be crazy to spend that kind of money buying machinery without knowing the details of what is required to make a product efficiently."*

In case of a production slow down, 40 percent of the manufacturing staff were working as temporaries doing all the operational transfers and process steps by hand. I was shocked to learn that many of them couldn't speak English and wondered how they could read and follow operating procedures.

I told them I needed to define what equipment was required to clean up the operation. Instead they ordered equipment anyway that was too flimsy for the task. Using sheet metal instead of sturdier stuff, the units looked like big refrigerators. The new lines required full time engineers to try to constantly make adjustments and keep up with repairs.

In ninety days, I determined what was required and that equipment would produce significantly better yields. Fortunately, the engineer in charge of the Asian manufacturing used the upgraded machinery I recommended and achieved greater yields than the production lines in Massachusetts and Colorado.

I also was surprised that shortly thereafter the engineering manager that hired me took a step backward to become an engineer again. He was suffering from burnout.

It appeared they also had assigned engineers several times who had no experience to solve their adhesive problems over the prior ten or twenty years. I was amazed they had electrical and mechanical engineers assigned to chemical process problems. There was no previous progress completed or reported during this period. They seemed to think that the 40 percent yield rate the industry was averaging was acceptable.

In the 1960s, an electronics engineer at a computer manufacturer said he, *"...could only help make computers, but didn't know how to use them for his design work."* With hundreds of transistors on a chip in the 1970s, computers were used for semiconductor design and piloting. The production line had daily reports on the computer terminals identifying production bottlenecks and output. So, computers were used in production as well. After twenty more years of making the computers, his company's products were the best in the marketplace, and he could use them for his planning and process requirements.

My company had the same problems initially but hadn't improved much in the 1990s when our division was purchased, and operations were moved to Asia. Since I had previously sold products to the computer industry, I'm flabbergasted that many computers on the market today work at all and for any length of time.

If I brought in all my technical magazines, books and supplier files I specifically needed at DEC from home, it would not leave room for a desk and chair in that small cubical. I couldn't be expected to remember everything, just where to look it up. Twenty years later, that same information still isn't available on the Internet. Having it on hand eliminated waiting for supplier literature and selection of samples needed to get a jump start on a new project.

As I tried to figure out how the Vax PC system made by Digital Equipment worked, I eventually learned that there were only about five people in the 5,000 local employees who could help me with any DEC computer problems. It seems many employees didn't read e-mails or P.C. reports (or know how to use the personal computers on their desktops).

After a while people would ask me, *"Why didn't you respond to my page?"*

I'd answer, *"I was at my desk, why didn't you call me?"*

I was told a condition of employment was pager use. I said, *"Nobody informed me of that when I was hired."*

They'd ask, *"Where is your pager?"*

I'd reply, *"There's one in my desk but it has no batteries."*

For an organisation where many employees didn't show up until 9 AM and would disappear by 3 PM, I wondered why they weren't losing more money than they were.

I was on-call to support manufacturing engineering 24 hours a day for seven days duration once every seven weeks. They called me at 2:00 AM one morning and said they had a manufacturing problem. I didn't understand why Manufacturing Engineering wasn't responsible for this kind of thing.

I went into work and asked, *"Okay, what's the problem?"*

They said, *"The parts failed inspection."*

I said, "How were they made?"

They said, "We don't know."

I asked, *"Who made them?"*

They didn't know.

I asked, *"Where are the manufacturing procedures?"*

They said, *"They're locked in the cabinet."*

I asked, *"Who has the key."*

They said, *"John, but he's on a trip."*

I went back home to bed.

Getting back to one of my original proposals, I made a thermoplastic adhesive film on a release carrier to replace the temporary one that would harden too much in the machine tooling process of the computer wafers. All those components had to be scrapped because they wouldn't separate cleanly from the tooling fixtures.

A new approach was needed to replace the thermoset paste adhesive which was smeared on with a spatula like a butter knife. The newly formulated hot melt film adhesive composite would be assembled like a grilled cheese sandwich and run through a conveyor oven to obtain a melt bond. This provided a uniform adhesive application that could be readily removed after the machining process.

The liquid version of the same new adhesive was applied with a computer-controlled syringe. It was similar to adhesive technology I had developed for use in aerospace and industrial applications. This alone improved the manufacturing yield over 30 percent and saved several million dollars a year.

Computer chip process trays would distort with heat and chips would fall out. Losing identification by location, the fallout parts could not be further processed. Trying a new, heat resistant moulded carrier with better chemical resistance was a big improvement. Upon delivery however, the new trays were warped. I developed a thermal process to relieve the moulded in stresses and flatten them out.

I also developed a method for electroplating the plastic carriers with metal that allowed the chips to dry faster in the process and applied for a patent.

The standard practice for fluid chip processing at high temperatures, involved analytical testing and certification of each reagent batch in one-gallon glass jugs. Switching to 55-gallon drums with a pump and an in-line filtration reduced the handling and costs while improving safety and reducing process time.

It so happened that my brother Jerry was leaving IBM. He was allowed to bring two guests for his retirement party. He invited his brother Russ from Wang Computers and his brother Tim from Digital Computers. His boss was probably surprised that we were all in the computer business at the time.

I was given an IBM pass for the event. The next day I put it on my bulletin board in my office. My boss did a double take when he saw the IBM badge at Digital Equipment with my name on it.

Eventually our group was sold to the Japanese and operations were moved to Asia. Hewlett Packard purchased part of what was left.

A few years later, I was astonished when I had four of my desktop computers crash on me in a ten-year period. Sometimes you just can't get good help to make products.

Chapter 36
Consulting Engineering

I've had many good bosses through the years and others who could make life difficult for people who were trying to get things done. I figured that since I knew how to do a lot of things in aerospace and industry, perhaps I should try my hand as an engineering consultant. I ended up doing a solo routine with certain clients and working with a partner or technical consulting groups at other times.

Examples include a programme involved developing textile coatings and laminates for auto interiors. Another was testing thermally conductive, non-metallic materials. Hot stamping foils and flexible fibre optics were done with a partner and a group respectively.

I worked with an engineering consulting firm on developing flame-resistant fibres for the military garments and shelters.

I had a partner in another group to scale up high temperature resistant, plastic canopies for planes. We rented equipment time at a consulting laboratory in Connecticut.

Because the new plastic powder was too fluffy as received from our chemist, it wouldn't feed through a screw-driven melt extruder (similar to a heated meat grinder). I made it denser by compacting the powder in a hydraulic press (like making a very large aspirin).

At a local kitchen appliance store I obtained a hand crank cheese grater. Going from a fluffy powder to small, compacted chunks fed the screw barrel in the hot extruder fast enough to make spaghetti like stands that could be chopped into pellets for sheet extrusion and injection moulding. We scaled that up operation with commercial sized grinding equipment.

Speaking of disclosing too much, I went to review an owner's company operation that was similar to that of a firm where we both were employed many years earlier. His general manager gave me a plant tour. I could tell he wasn't too happy about an outsider asking too many questions and me volunteering suggestions on increasing production rates. When I told the owner where improvements and corrections could be made, he was thrilled.

I suspect I wasn't issued a follow up contract because his general manager was threatened by my feedback and said he could do it himself.

Another client was losing customers (and major sales dollars) in Europe for ghosting and haze forming on their photocopy films. This had been going on for some time and they had no idea of the cause.

I wrote up a detailed report describing the cause of the problem and how to rectify it. I brought in the report along with an invoice for the time spent. After I was paid, they weren't returning my calls. Some months later, they said, *"We tried your recommendations ourselves and you were right. They solved the problem."*

I never got another request to help them again. Apparently, they didn't compare the small cost of my expertise with the amount of savings on rejected product and lost sales revenues.

Chapter 37
Slowing Down to a Whoa

While I was building up my customer base as a technical consultant, I moved into a new home in the same town. After closing on the house, I was going to put boxes into the attic over the garage for storage. A February snowstorm was predicted the next day and I wanted to make room to get the cars into the garage.

The fold-down stairs to the garage attic storage collapsed when I was at the top. I hadn't noticed the stairs were only tacked in place with a few wire brads (small finish nails).

Obviously, the town building inspector and the general contractor didn't inspect the attic of the finished house after the carpenter subcontractor failed to complete the installation of the stairs. Apparently, the realtor couldn't be held responsible for strongly recommending the builder once she had pocketed her commission.

On the way down to the cement floor, my head broke the cast aluminium table attachment on my bandsaw. The cement floor fractured my tailbone and compressed my spine on the 13-foot fall.

I waited over six hours to get X-rays, only to be told I had to lie on my back for some of them. Everything hurt, but the whole back was the worst. I didn't understand why they couldn't take the pictures with me lying face down, but at least they finished with me standing up. They stapled my scalp together and gave me pain pills before sending me home.

I lost an inch of height because my spine is still compressed which retards the flow of spinal fluid (not a good thing). My nerves still remain damaged over twenty years later. Surgical removal of the broken end of my tailbone offered no relief from the back pain and the base of my spine still swells up.

Too many pain and antidepressant pills were prescribed that didn't help. Most doctors either said they couldn't help or find anything wrong. A world-renowned Boston neurologist tested me for five hours with things like third grade math and simple logic. He couldn't suggest a treatment for improvement in thinking.

Besides all the headaches and pain, I'd lost a significant amount of my long and short-term memory. Not knowing when I was going to have a good day, I wouldn't be reliable to work on an assignment for technical clients unless they were in no hurry for solutions.

Finally, an interventional radiologist prescribed a steroid shot into the right sacral-iliac joint two years later. A month after I was feeling slightly better, so I accepted a research and development position in New Hampshire. I assumed I was on the road to recovery and would be able to work full time again.

Chapter 38
Foss Manufacturing

A specialty fibre extrusion firm in Hampden, NH manufactured needled felt textiles, matts and composites. I found that if I drove up from Massachusetts on a Monday and was laying down to rest every minute I was not at work; I could function for a full 40 hours per week. Then I'd drive home on Friday for the weekend. Fortunately, I was travelling both ways against the heavy vacation traffic that was not moving in the other direction on the interstate highways.

We made interior laminates for automobiles, busses and recreational vehicles. Many of the non-woven textiles were used in shoes, clothing and boots.

I applied for patents on antibiotic treatments for fabrics and a conductive coating for electrostatic charge dissipation in clean rooms while I was at Foss Manufacturing. One problem in measuring low order conductivity accurately was that the equipment necessary for direct testing cost several thousand dollars. I went to Radio Shack and purchased a good multimeter for $75 instead to be able to calculate the numbers.

I was referred to "*the best orthopaedic back surgeon in New Hampshire*" by the company president. Three months out was the soonest I could get an appointment. I had to drive an hour across the state to see him and spent another hour in his waiting room. He charged me $177 for a five-minute visit.

He asked me, "*What did they do for you in your back surgery?*"

I said, "*They removed the broken tip of my tail bone.*"

He said, "*I don't recommend that. Did it help?*"

I said, "*No.*"

He said, "*See!*" Then he said, "*There is no surgery I could perform to help.*"

Because I was getting worse, I returned for another steroid shot in Massachusetts. They did the same thing in the same place again without achieving the same benefits as the first shot. I continued to go downhill mentally and physically over the five-month period to the point where I couldn't work at all anymore and had to resign.

Chapter 39
Recovery

In reality, I couldn't function well for a dozen years after I fell. As I learned to tolerate pain better and was regaining some of my long and short-term memory, I found a Doctor of Osteopathy who helped me gradually improve physically over the next five years or so.

The only thing I could do at my own pace was write. As long as I kept stopping and changing positions frequently, I could handle the pain. The next few years I attended creative writing classes, writers' workshops and writing seminars.

I had always been able to rhyme words easily without paying attention to rhythm. I did submit a poem in iambic pentameter that was published in a book of poems called '*Sunflowers and Seashells*'. I found that poetry is exceptionally limiting when the words needed to rhyme detract from the meaning to be conveyed. On the other hand, I've never understood how they can call prose that doesn't rhyme a poem. The non-rhyming 'poems' I've read seem to be poor prose at that and only ramble on and on.

I had two mystery book releases before my publisher went out of business. Both were based on world events from recent years. Without the marketing programme the publisher had promised, I received limited feedback, not to mention a lack of royalties on the books sold. The sporadic comments coming in were very encouraging though. I started to write this memoir about the effort to put man on the moon, before I return to writing novels. The tentative title of my new mystery is MUESLI MURDERS because Cereal Killer had already been used.

Chapter 40
Aerospace Engineers – Where to Find Them

Ross Perot, founder of Electronic Data Systems and a former independent candidate for President of the United States, said in his book, "*Eagles don't flock, you have to find them one at a time ...*"

We found the same to be true to sift out the truly talented people to support NASA's efforts in the race with the Soviets to get to the moon first.

Earlier I mentioned that after working on high-altitude flight, full pressure suits for the US Air Force and Gemini spacesuits for NASA at the David Clark Company in Worcester, MA, I left for work at GE's Plastics Division. General Electric was scaling up manufacture on new, high performance engineering polymers (plastics) in upstate (Selkirk) New York. Our continued employment offers to move from Pittsfield, Massachusetts didn't include sufficient financial inducement to cover the increased cost of living in the greater Albany area. Most of us in the Plastics Division chose to leave the company.

When David Clark Co. in Worcester, MA lost the Apollo Block II contract to International Latex's Government and Industrial Division (now called ILC Dover) several former Clark employees were recruited to the Delaware location.

ILC was awarded a NASA construction contract on a suit concept. It still needed to be fully defined and proven in a very short timeline that it could withstand the ten mission cycles envisioned without failure.

Goodrich Corporation in Akron, Ohio had also invested considerable time and effort in developing an alternative suit concept to protect the astronauts from the extreme environments in space and on the lunar surface. They ended up as bridesmaids in the bidding process. Obviously, certain people at Goodrich were candidates at ILC Dover because they had detailed knowledge of the programme requirements. They could hit the ground running as soon as they came on board.

ILC urgently required additional engineering staff to scale up for the Apollo contract. They made arrangements with LTV (Ling-Temco-Vought Aerospace Corporation in Texas) to rent select skilled aerospace engineers and chemists while ILC expanded their work force.

The approach also works in reverse to locate the right people or have them find you. I was telling a friend how I happened to end up working for Dennison Manufacturing in Framingham, MA before they merged to become Avery Dennison.

I said, *"I contacted a chemist at Dennison Stationary Products who worked on the Apollo Program at Owens Corning Fiberglass facility in Ashton, RI."*

He referred me to Dr West, the General Manager of Corporate R&D who sent me to Dick, the general manager of Corporate Advanced Development. When I walked in for my first interview, I looked at my future boss and said, *"Boy, are you in trouble."*

I explained that the head of Dennison's personnel office had contacted me. She was offended to be left out of the hiring loop. Dick said, *"It doesn't matter. I'll talk to her later."*

As it turned out, she had no idea what was involved and wasn't up to speed to evaluate my qualifications for a position that hadn't as yet been defined.

Dick then sent me to meet his boss Dr Lewis, the Corporate Executive Vice President of Technology.

Henry interviewed me to discuss the possibility of having me manage everything in Advanced Development except for the company's high speed, ion deposition printing business. The new group would be called New Chemical Technologies to work on corporate new product efforts and assist the divisions with their research and development programmes.

After I was hired, I defined projects as I settled in and talked to the different divisions. Along the way, I put on professional development seminars for the corporate technical people. As an incentive, I used books written by the presenters of each topic (such as project management) as an incentive for perfect attendance at the meetings. I was also appointed to the patent review committee.

That's kind of the way almost all my position hires at other firms went – without involvement of human resources, except for explanation of company benefits, rules, guidelines, etc. Typically, they didn't know what was going on and were not qualified to evaluate the backgrounds of technical candidates.

The same process worked for people I've hired through the years. I also never found a useful head-hunter when I was looking for people. I frequently would talk to business associates, suppliers and customers for recommendations.

When Avery Dennison was closing down the Framingham, Massachusetts facility, I was asked to go to Avery's Corporate Research and Development facility in Pasadena, California. When I turned that down, there was noise about me not being allowed to work for an Avery Dennison competitor.

Instead I went to Digital Equipment since they were less than five miles from home. To locate people in DEC, I contacted a chief engineer at their headquarters in Maynard, MA who I done work for years before as a potential supplier. He sent me to the Digital Equipment Corporation location in Shrewsbury, MA facility with a strong recommendation.

Chapter 41
Summary

It would be nice if the moral of this story on the United States space programmes was, "It was so easy, anyone could do it." That was far from being the case. Fortunately, we found enough Americans with *'the right stuff'* to present a united front and get the whole job done to pass the Russians in their aerospace effort in the process. I still feel good when I see something that I designed, invented or fixed fifty years ago still in use today.

Other industries, such as the auto manufacturers of the 1970s, were satisfied with a partial solution and would throw a concept into production before it was ready. They decided to cut back on their quality departments and let the customers test and have it 'fixed' later at their dealers. This is also true of the computer industry where software products are modified for different end user markets after the sale.

From the development examples contained herein, it can be seen that learning needs to be an ongoing process over a lifetime. In order to solve problems efficiently and invent new answers, one must draw from life's total experiences and background.

Confined to only what has been done in that particular field of study ignores alternative options found in other technologies. With a twist or spin, new uses for a wheel con be derived from another industry or application without taking time to reinvent a different type of wheel. Discovery can come from personal experience, summer jobs growing up, education and training besides staying current with advances in other diverse technologies.

I had an engineering professor who worked in industry during school breaks. He said he made more money during the summer than he netted for the rest of the year, but he loved teaching. He brought a wealth of information to class based on his industrial experience in addition to covering the traditional texts and providing stimulating lectures on the subject. Most of his exams were open book. If you didn't know where to look up the answer or how to use the engineering formulations, data and tables, there was not sufficient time to complete the test.

After the last lunar landing (Apollo 17), there was a glut of aerospace engineers in the job market. Except for favouritism and company politics, the people with sub-par or marginal performance were the first to be let go from the space programmes. That created a feeling that these particular engineers and scientists couldn't make the transition to perform well in an industrial environment.

Having been in and out of three different space programmes (Gemini, Apollo and Shuttle), I can attest that industrial, aerospace, military, commercial and life's experiences have technologies that are readily interchangeable and transferrable to other fields.

WISPA

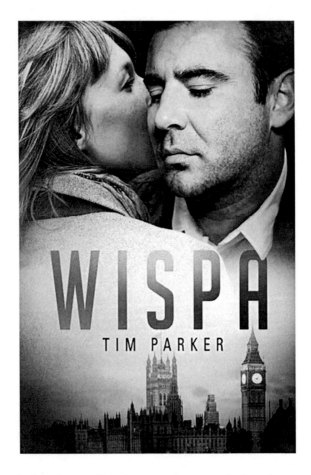

The Author has written two mystery novels based on recent world events:

A workaholic vice president of finance on Wall Street decides to take a little time off to attend her college reunion in the foothills of the Berkshire Mountains. In an off-campus diner, Pam encounters a disabled combat veteran teaching at the university. Sparks begin to fly as they get to know each other. Pam tries to resign her position to be with Jake. He seems wonderful, if not a bit quirky, but red flags start to crop up. At last Jake reveals he is working undercover for Homeland Security to prevent millions of people from being poisoned in New England. Subsequent to a background check, the CIA asks Pam if she will help them find ways to identify cells planning attacks against Americans. While on vacation overseas, they are assailed by fanatics, return to North America and go into hiding. Because of their efforts, jihad plots are also foiled in Canadian oil fields and against the underground trains in England. They assume new identities to resume their lives as civilians but can't work together in case the terrorists are still looking for them.

MISSING

MISSING in Switzerland

Peter Pickering, a British businessman working for the CIA, disappeared in Switzerland. His wife, Monique asked detective Tom Powers to find him. Pickering, a distributor of components for durable goods, was recruited to stop the drain of United States technology for use in weapons by terrorists. Peter's wife, Monique, hired Tom to find Peter, who failed to meet her in Amsterdam after a Zurich business trip.

Ultimately, Peter turned up with amnesia as a John Doe left for dead in Germany. Pickering's journal was missing, which may have contained clues about who attacked him and why. Tom was shot by an intruder at the client's home in the Berkshires protecting CIA agent Joan Walters.

The investigators travelled to Europe for answers but encountered spies who killed one of Peter's Zurich customers and ransacked his office. Tom's life was saved by the young agent who took down one of the spies and captured the other who were seeking American technology secrets.

Tom and Joan then became more than partners working in Switzerland to stop the flow of arms to terrorists and rogue nations.

The contributions to this memoir by Natalie Spinetti, Sue Strelow and Jerry Parker are acknowledged with many thanks for their diligence, tolerance, patience and help.

"My colleagues and I have agreed that your autobiographical work is well-written and offers an insightful look into your life working on developing spacesuits."
James Houghton, Editor, Olympia Publishers, London

"One of the most fascinating interviews I've done in a long time – I learned a lot in the process."
Kevin Flanders, Author
Writer – Stonebridge Press

"Your work is was well written and enthralling as it encompasses behind-the-scenes information. Readers will find the details throughout this work to be informative."
Austin Macauley Publishers, NYC

"Your book is an intriguing and insightful read, particularly as it comes from an authoritative first person."
David Learner, Executive Editor
AMP, London

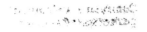